# KINGDOM DISCIPLES

BIBLE STUDY

# TONY EVANS

## HEAVEN'S
## REPRESENTATIVES
## ON EARTH

LifeWay Press® • Nashville, Tennessee

## Editorial Team

Reid Patton
*Content Editor*

David Haney
*Production Editor*

Jon Rodda
*Art Director*

Joel Polk
*Editorial Team Leader*

Brian Daniel
*Manager, Short-Term Discipleship*

Michael Kelley
*Director, Groups Ministry*

Published by LifeWay Press® • © 2018 Tony Evans

No part of this book may be reproduced or transmitted in any form or by any means, electronic or mechanical, including photocopying and recording, or by any information storage or retrieval system, except as may be expressly permitted in writing by the publisher. Requests for permission should be addressed in writing to LifeWay Press®; One LifeWay Plaza; Nashville, TN 37234.

ISBN 978-1-4158-7202-4 • Item 005469851

Dewey decimal classification: 248.5
Subject headings: DISCIPLESHIP \ EVANGELISTIC WORK \ KINGDOM OF GOD

Unless indicated otherwise, Scripture quotations are taken from the New American Standard Bible®, Copyright © 1960, 1962, 1963, 1968, 1971, 1972, 1973, 1975, 1977, 1995 by The Lockman Foundation. Used by permission. (www.lockman.org). Scripture quotations marked KJV are from the Holy Bible, King James Version.

To order additional copies of this resource, write to LifeWay Resources Customer Service; One LifeWay Plaza; Nashville, TN 37234; fax 615-251-5933; call toll free 800-458-2772; order online at LifeWay.com; email orderentry@lifeway.com; or visit the LifeWay Christian Store serving you.

*Printed in the United States of America*

Groups Ministry Publishing • LifeWay Resources • One LifeWay Plaza • Nashville, TN 37234

# CONTENTS

# THE AUTHOR

**DR. TONY EVANS** is one of America's most respected leaders in evangelical circles. He is a pastor, a best-selling author, and a frequent speaker at Bible conferences and seminars throughout the nation.

Dr. Evans has served as the senior pastor of Oak Cliff Bible Fellowship for more than forty years, witnessing its growth from ten people in 1976 to more than ten thousand congregants with more than one hundred ministries.

Dr. Evans also serves as the president of The Urban Alternative, a national ministry that seeks to bring about spiritual renewal in America through the church. His daily radio broadcast, "The Alternative with Dr. Tony Evans," can be heard on more than thirteen hundred radio outlets throughout the United States and in more than 130 countries.

Dr. Evans has authored more than one hundred books, including *Oneness Embraced, The Kingdom Agenda, Marriage Matters, Kingdom Man, Victory in Spiritual Warfare, It's Not Too Late, Horizontal Jesus, The Power of God's Names, Detours,* and *Kingdom Disciples.* Dr. Evans, a former chaplain for the NFL Dallas Cowboys, is currently the chaplain for the NBA's Dallas Mavericks, a team he has served for more than thirty years.

Through his local church and national ministry, Dr. Evans has set in motion a kingdom-agenda philosophy of ministry that teaches God's comprehensive rule over every area of life, as demonstrated through the individual, family, church, and society.

Dr. Evans is married to Lois, his wife and ministry partner of more than forty years. They are the proud parents of four: Chrystal, Priscilla, Anthony Jr., and Jonathan.

# INTRODUCTION

Cradled within the depths of all that defines our humanity lies an unyielding fascination with kingdom. No matter what color, creed, or culture we examine, even the most cursory glance into the annals and accounts passed down either by pen or by tongue reveals something intertwined with kingdom. Whether it's the great kings of Scripture, such as David and Solomon, or whether it's rulers like Caesar, Alexander the Great, Charlemagne, and Tutankhamen, the leaders of kingdoms captivate us, intriguing our imaginations.

Even rulers who didn't hold the official title of king have left their legacies, for good or for bad, to enthrall us. Napoleon, the dominator of continental Europe, possessed a formidable intellect and a superior military mind. For several hundred years the pharaohs used their considerable strength and skill to advance Egypt beyond the other nations in academics, engineering, medicine, and writing. The monarchs, spanning more than sixteen hundred years of history, ruled over what humbly began as the Angles, then Aengla Land, and eventually what we know today as England.

Stories of conquerors, conquests, rebellions, and conspiracies mesmerize us. We tell them to our children in fairy tales riddled with kings, queens, princes, princesses, and kingdoms. The life of a king or a queen is often envied. Yet that envy is naïve. As the playwright William Shakespeare wrote, "Uneasy lies the head that wears the crown."[1] Kings, queens, and rulers frequently function in a culture of conflict, even violence. As a result, history reminds us again and again, through what may seem like the same story set on a different stage, that kings and rulers often resort to extreme measures to protect their personal interests and power.

Nowhere in any story of a king or a kingdom do we read about the ruler himself sacrificing his greatest treasure simply for the benefit of others. Sure, sacrifices were made. But always toward the aim of preserving power rather than yielding it.

That is, except for the one true King who gave up His own Son, Jesus Christ, so that those who believed on Him—His death, burial, and resurrection—would be restored to a place of fellowship and dominion with their King, a position they had lost in the battle of the garden.

The King gave His life so that we could gain access to His kingdom. He offered His example for us to follow and emulate. Under His rule we're called to the highest position as heirs to His inheritance, freely granted to us when we follow Him as a true kingdom disciple. Let's explore together what it means to live all of life under the comprehensive rule of God, gaining all the access and authority designed for royalty.

1. William Shakespeare, *History of Henry IV,* act 3, scene 1, line 1735, *Open Source Shakespeare,* accessed November 10, 2017, http://opensourceshakespeare.org/views/plays/play_view. php?WorkID=henry4p2&Act=3&Scene=1&Scope=scene.

# How to Use This Study

*This Bible-study book includes six weeks of content for group and personal study.*

## Group Experience

Regardless of what day of the week your group meets, each week of content begins with the group session. Each group session uses the following format to facilitate simple yet meaningful interaction among group members, with God's Word, and with the teaching of Dr. Evans.

### Start

This page includes questions to get the conversation started and to introduce the video segment.

### Watch

This page includes key points from Dr. Evans's teaching, along with blanks for taking notes as participants watch the video.

### Discuss

This page includes questions and statements that guide the group to respond to Dr. Evans's video teaching and to relevant Bible passages.

## Personal Experience

Each week provides five days of Bible study and learning activities for individual engagement between group sessions. The personal study revisits stories, Scriptures, and themes Dr. Evans introduced in the videos so that participants can understand and apply them on a personal level. The days are numbered 1–5 to provide personal reading and activities for each day of the week, leaving two days off to worship with your church family and to meet as a small group. If your group meets on the same day as your worship gathering, use the extra day to reflect on what God is teaching you and to practice putting the biblical principles into action.

# TIPS FOR LEADING A SMALL GROUP

*Follow these guidelines to prepare for each group session.*

## PRAYERFULLY PREPARE

### REVIEW

Review the weekly material and group questions ahead of time.

### PRAY

Be intentional about praying for each person in the group.

Ask the Holy Spirit to work through you and the group discussion as you point to Jesus each week through God's Word.

## MINIMIZE DISTRACTIONS

Create a comfortable environment. If group members are uncomfortable, they'll be distracted and therefore not engaged in the group experience. Plan ahead by considering these details:

### SEATING

### TEMPERATURE

### LIGHTING

### FOOD OR DRINK

### SURROUNDING NOISE

### GENERAL CLEANLINESS

At best, thoughtfulness and hospitality show guests and group members they're welcome and valued in whatever environment you choose to gather. At worst, people may never notice your effort, but they're also not distracted. Do everything in your ability to help people focus on what's most important: connecting with God, with the Bible, and with one another.

# INCLUDE OTHERS

Your goal is to foster a community in which people are welcome just as they are but encouraged to grow spiritually. Always be aware of opportunities to include any people who visit the group and to invite new people to join your group.

An inexpensive way to make first-time guests feel welcome or to invite someone to get involved is to give them their own copies of this Bible-study book.

# ENCOURAGE DISCUSSION

A good small-group experience has the following characteristics.

## EVERYONE PARTICIPATES
Encourage everyone to ask questions, share responses, or read aloud.

## NO ONE DOMINATES—NOT EVEN THE LEADER
Be sure that your time speaking as a leader takes up less than half of your time together as a group. Politely guide discussion if anyone dominates.

## NOBODY IS RUSHED THROUGH QUESTIONS
Don't feel that a moment of silence is a bad thing. People often need time to think about their responses to questions they've just heard or to gain courage to share what God is stirring in their hearts.

## INPUT IS AFFIRMED AND FOLLOWED UP
Make sure you point out something true or helpful in a response. Don't just move on. Build community with follow-up questions, asking how other people have experienced similar things or how a truth has shaped their understanding of God and the Scripture you're studying. People are less likely to speak up if they fear that you don't actually want to hear their answers or that you're looking for only a certain answer.

## GOD AND HIS WORD ARE CENTRAL
Opinions and experiences can be helpful, but God has given us the truth. Trust God's Word to be the authority and God's Spirit to work in people's lives. You can't change anyone, but God can. Continually point people to the Word and to active steps of faith.

# KEEP CONNECTING

Think of ways to connect with group members during the week. Participation during the group session is always improved when members spend time connecting with one another outside the group sessions. The more people are comfortable with and involved in one another's lives, the more they'll look forward to being together. When people move beyond being friendly to truly being friends who form a community, they come to each session eager to engage instead of merely attending.

Encourage group members with thoughts, commitments, or questions from the session by connecting through these communication channels:

### EMAILS

### TEXTS

### SOCIAL MEDIA

When possible, build deeper friendships by planning or spontaneously inviting group members to join you outside your regularly scheduled group time for activities like these:

### MEALS

### FUN ACTIVITIES

### PROJECTS AROUND YOUR HOME, CHURCH, OR COMMUNITY

Week One

# THE MISSING KEY

*Group Experience*

# START

*Welcome to session 1 of* Kingdom Disciples. *Begin by taking a few minutes to be sure everyone knows one another, especially if this is your first time to meet as a group.*

**What sources of authority lead and influence the way you live?**

**How do these authorities shape the decisions you make?**

All people live under the rules and guidance of authority. Whether that authority is a local or national governing authority or a supervisor at work, we all know what it means to live under the authority of another person. For kingdom disciples, the ruling and reigning authority is Jesus Christ. In this session Dr. Evans will talk about what it means to be kingdom disciples who bring Jesus' authority to bear on the world around us.

Before we learn what Dr. Evans has to teach us about being a kingdom disciple, would somebody pray for our time together, asking the Lord to open our hearts and minds to His Word as we begin this study?

 # WATCH

*Refer to this viewer guide as you watch video session 1.*

### KINGDOM DISCIPLE

A believer in Christ who takes part in the spiritual-development process of progressively learning how to live all of their lives under the lordship of Jesus Christ

Worshiping God is the recognition of who He is, what He has done, and what you are trusting Him to do.

*Authority* means "power in legitimate hands."

The purpose of the Book of Matthew is to demonstrate that Jesus Christ is King.

The word *make disciples* is an imperative, which means it's a command; it's not a request.

Disciples are transformed people who transfer the values of the kingdom of God.

### THREE WAYS TO MAKE DISCIPLES

1. Go.      2. Baptize them.      3. Teach them.

Go and deliver the fact that Jesus Christ has come and that He has come with authority.

Baptism is your place of identification.

The purpose of teaching is to understand or to learn what it means to be a representative.

You are learning the Word of God in order to use the Word of God to express the authority of the Word of God as the representative of the lordship of Jesus Christ as a kingdom disciple.

When you are a kingdom disciple and a kingdom-disciple maker, you get more experience of Jesus Christ than if you are not.

 # DISCUSS

*Discuss the video with your group, using these questions.*

How would you define what it means to be a disciple?

Read Matthew 28:19. What does it mean to make disciples? What distinction did Dr. Evans make between Christians and kingdom disciples?

A kingdom disciple understands that Jesus is King and that He rules. What's the relationship between discipleship and the authority of Jesus?

Jesus wants us to emulate not only His person but also His authority. What happens when we emulate Jesus' person without His authority?

Who or what besides Jesus do people look to as the ultimate authority in their lives?

Why do we treat the Great Commission like a polite request instead of an authoritative command?

Dr. Evans compared the authority of Christ to that of an official controlling a ball game. The problem today is that too many Christians have neglected their God-given authority and joined teams on the field. What are some teams you've joined that threaten your officiating responsibility in God's kingdom?

Dr Evans said, "Baptism means more than getting someone wet. It means being identified." What are some other ways you identify with Christ in your daily life?

Describe a time when you saw God show up in a powerful way in the process of making disciples.

What would change about our community if this group of believers committed to extending Jesus' authority into the world around us?

*Read week 1 and complete the activities before the next group session.*

# KINGDOM LIVING

Jesus plainly spoke of His kingdom when He told Pilate that its ways don't reflect the ways of the kingdoms on earth:

> Jesus answered, "My kingdom is not of this world.
> If My kingdom were of this world, then My servants
> would be fighting so that I would not be handed over
> to the Jews; but as it is, My kingdom is not of this realm."
> JOHN 18:36

Jesus' kingdom is a kingdom without borders and a kingdom without time. To try and apply the rules, precepts, and writs of this world to this very unearthly kingdom would be similar to bringing a horse and a polo stick to an NFL linebacker on a football field and instructing him to play. The rules and tools of this earth don't govern the rules of God's kingdom. As the King, God sets the way His kingdom is to operate and function.

For example, in God's kingdom, neither race nor gender delineates inequality. In His kingdom, power goes to the weak who recognize their weakness and humbly look to Him. Forgiveness preeminently reigns, and the amount of money matters less than the heart that offers it, as we see in the case of the widow's mite (see Mark 12:41-44). Significance in this unusual kingdom is connected to service.

By the Holy Spirit, the story of this unique kingdom has been preserved for us, its subjects—kingdom disciples of the Lord Jesus Christ—in the Bible. Throughout Scripture, chroniclers inspired by the Spirit recorded; encouraged; equipped; lamented; and presented the history, rules, redemption, and purpose of our King and His kingdom.

Unfortunately, many of us today are living in the realm of a King we also seek to dethrone. We subtly undermine His reign through expressions of complacency; autonomy; independence; or simply a lack of connection to Him, His Word, His laws, and His covenants. As a result, we experience in our personal lives, homes, churches, communities, and nation the chaos that comes from rebellion.

In a kingdom, life is to be lived under the rule and authority of the King. The blessings of the covenant charter of our King in His Word, the authority He gives us through the dominion covenant (see Gen. 1:26-28), His promises, and His *chesed* love come only when we live all of life under God's rule as His disciples.

## Day One

# WHAT IS A KINGDOM DISCIPLE?

Welcome to your journey to become a full-fledged disciple of our King. Kingdom disciples are in short supply these days. The result has been a bevy of powerless Christians who attend powerless churches that embody a powerless presence in the world.

Until we return to lives of discipleship, we'll continue to fail in our calling to live as heaven's representatives on earth. This is because the power, authority, abundance, victory, and impact promised in God's Word to His people is ours only when we align ourselves under Him as His disciples. Until then we can anticipate that chaos and crisis will continue to reign supreme in spite of all the Christian activities we engage in, Christian books we read, Christian songs we sing, and small groups we join.

Discipleship is a very personal decision. It starts when a person commits himself or herself to God as His follower and allows the results of that commitment to overflow into everything else in life.

**What's the difference between a disciple and a convert?**

**What are some ways you believe a kingdom disciple lives out that role? List some practical outcomes in a person's life.**

Surrender to Christ's lordship and obedience to His rule of love unlock God's power to bring heaven to bear on earth. A kingdom disciple lives out this divine power and influence. I define *kingdom disciple* this way:

A believer in Christ who takes part in the spiritual-developmental
process of progressively learning to live all of life under the lordship
of Jesus

The goal of kingdom disciples is to live transformed lives that transfer the values
of the kingdom of God to earth so that they replicate themselves in the lives of
others. The result of such replication is God's exercising His rule and His authority
from heaven to history through His kingdom disciples.

**Read Matthew 28:19. What's the central focus of this verse?**

**Define what it means to make a disciple.**

**Can you make disciples without first being a disciple yourself?
Why or why not?**

Matthew 28:18 says:

> Jesus came up and spoke to them, saying, "All authority
> has been given to Me in heaven and on earth."
> Matthew 28:18

The word translated as *authority* in the English version of this verse essentially means "power, right, liberty, jurisdiction, and strength." *Strong's Concordance* reveals that this term denotes "power of choice" or "doing as one pleases," even "the power of judicial decisions."[1] When Jesus said all authority was His in heaven and on earth, He was saying that He possesses the legal right to use that power.

Power without authority matters little. Take, for example, NFL players. They're far more powerful than the older referees officiating the game. Yet they exercise that power only under the authority of the referees. If they choose to misuse their power, a referee simply throws out a flag. If the player persists in wrongly using his power, the referee can then eject him from the game altogether.

When Jesus said all authority had been given to Him, that authority encompassed not only power but also the right to use that power as He chose.

**Read Job 1:12. What boundaries were placed on Satan with regard to Job?**

**How does God's authority place limits on the way Satan exercises His power? Why are these limits important for us to recognize?**

**List two primary differences between Satan's limited power and Jesus' boundless authority.**

**1.**

**2.**

Power is someone's ability to influence another person through strength, personality, control, or deception. Authority, on the other hand, is someone's legitimate, vested, and formal right to wield power. Enormous difference exists between the two realities, but when we fail to discern this difference, we can foolishly choose to fight power with power (rather than authority) or seek to live by our own power (rather than the authority given to us in Christ).

When Jesus was tested in the wilderness (see Matt. 4:1-11), Satan's power was outmatched by Jesus' authority. After being offered temptations of power and fulfillment in this world, Jesus appealed to the full, final authority He possessed as the Son of God.

In other words, Satan has been given power only on earth. Unfortunately, far too many believers seek to overcome his tactics or fight his attacks in their own power. But that will never work. That's why we've been instructed never to rebuke Satan on our own and with our own skills (see Eph. 6:12-18) but rather to resist him (see Jas. 4:7) and to rebuke him only in the authority of Jesus' name (see Zech. 3:2; Jude 9).

When you understand the importance of authority, you'll grow as a kingdom disciple to the point that you can not only resist the devil but also call on heaven, as Jesus did, to bear in your earthly endeavors.

**Refer to Jesus' temptation in Matthew 4:1-11. What are some ways we take hold of heaven's authority and make it ours?**

**Read John 10:17-18. How far does Christ's authority reach? How does recognizing the extent of His authority bring you comfort and a sense of security?**

If you've never differentiated between power and authority, let that sink in. Jesus offers you complete authority in Him when you live as His disciple. Many powers are coming against you that are stronger than you could ever be on your own, but He has overcome the world (see John 16:33). Consider the comfort and peace that come from knowing you have access to the authority of the Creator of the universe. Let that reality motivate you to grow as a disciple of the King.

**Where do you most need Jesus' power and authority in your life today?**

## *Prayer*

Heavenly Father, thank You for this Bible study
on power, authority, and discipleship. I commit
my study to You and ask that You'll surround my days,
thoughts, activities, and actions in such a way that this
study will be a priority for me. In Christ's name, amen.

---

1. Strong's G1849, Blue Letter Bible, accessed December 12, 2017, https://www.blueletterbible.org/lang/lexicon/lexicon.cfm?Strongs=G1849&t=NASB.

# Day Two
# SALVATION AND DISCIPLESHIP

According to Jesus, a disciple's first concern should be for God's will to be done on earth just as it's done in heaven (see Matt. 6:10). How is God's will done in heaven? Completely and perfectly, with no questions, no objections, and no debate. In fact, Satan was the only one ever to challenge God's will in heaven, and he was therefore banished.

Jesus' plan in making disciples is to establish a group of people who function as His legal representatives by reflecting and implementing God's authority and will on earth. This is our role and responsibility as kingdom disciples. The discipleship process is designed to transfer Jesus' authority to and through His followers. That way observing the lives of believers individually and collectively gives a glimpse into the activity of heaven.

Christians are to exercise heaven's authority in history. Kingdom discipleship and authority go hand in hand. Sometimes we miss this fact because discipleship and authority aren't usually taught as complementary ideas. But as a kingdom disciple, you're uniquely positioned as an extension of God's legitimate authority in heaven so that His will and work are done on earth. That's a very important calling.

**Read Luke 9:1-2. What did Jesus give His disciples authority over and authority to do?**

**Jesus is the same yesterday, today, and tomorrow (see Heb. 13:8). The authority He has provided for us as His disciples is the same as well. Why do you think so many disciples fail to exercise the type of authority Jesus gave us?**

**Because Jesus has already achieved victory and Satan is a defeated enemy, what's our role as Jesus' followers on earth?**

The purpose of the church and of each individual believer is to make disciples, not just add names to the church roll or increase Bible-study attendance. It's not enough for the church just to be open a certain number of hours a week or offer a variety of programs. We're to make disciples. Only by making disciples can we reflect God's rule in history. Each time a disciple is made, God is robbing the domain of darkness and making someone His own. Jesus described this as entering the house of a strongman (Satan) and carrying off His property (see Matt. 12:29). People who respond to the call of salvation reflect God's rule in the world.

**What can Christians do more intentionally, either corporately or individually, to make disciples?**

**Have you ever thought about discipleship as a means God uses to establish His authority on earth? Why or why not?**

There's a distinction between a person's salvation and discipleship. Evangelism ought to carry a large emphasis in our churches and our personal lives, but the Christian life experience doesn't end at salvation. Salvation is just the beginning. Everyone who's saved should then grow as a disciple.

Salvation is absolutely free (see Rev. 22:17), and entrance into the kingdom is ensured forever when you place your faith in the finished work of Jesus Christ and His promise to give eternal life to all who trust in Him (see John 5:24; 6:47). But becoming a kingdom disciple demands submission and surrender to the lordship of Jesus Christ in every area of life. Surrendering to Jesus' lordship means you choose to spend your time, talents, and treasure for God and His glory rather than your own.

The level to which you grow and live as a disciple will have a direct effect on your inheritance in the kingdom as well. While entrance into the kingdom is ensured through the finished work of Christ, your rewards will be determined by the degree of faithfulness with which you serve the King as His disciple here and now. (see Matt. 25:20-23; 1 Cor. 3:8).

**In your own words, describe the difference between salvation and discipleship.**

**Why is it important to understand that while entrance into heaven is secured through Jesus' sacrificial death, your inheritance in heaven rests on your responsibility as a disciple on earth?**

**In what way should that understanding affect your behavior?**

Calling demands that we change the way we live. Becoming a Christian is without a cost, but becoming a kingdom disciple demands a cost. We understand that commitment comes with a cost. Years ago when the military draft was still in operation, young men were often called into the service at very inopportune times. For example, it didn't matter if you had just gotten married. It was goodbye, bride; hello, Uncle Sam. The same was true if the draftee just got a great job. But this new draftee did more than just leave family and friends behind. He now became the property of the U.S. government. His new master dictated every detail of his life: when to get up or go to bed; what to eat; even how to dress, stand, and walk.

After boot camp the military took a further step in controlling the soldier's life. It selected a new location for him, usually far from home, and a new occupation. If the nation was at war, this soldier could be sent to the front line, where he might be killed in the line of duty.

If young men could be expected to sacrifice everything for their country, how much more should we as believers be willing to do whatever our Commander, Jesus Christ, asks of us? That's what's expected of us as His followers.

**Read Mark 8:35-36 aloud. Substitute the words *a man* and *his* in verse 36 with personal pronouns for yourself. What does it mean to "gain the whole world" yet "forfeit" your soul?**

**In light of the fact that salvation is already yours through Jesus' sacrifice, what did He mean when He said if you lose your life for His sake, you'll gain it?**

How do you gain the whole world yet lose your life? By pursuing temporal realities that don't last. A lifetime is only a moment on an eternal measuring line. When you accumulate things that last only these few moments on earth, you're forfeiting rewards and inheritance that will last forever. And in this world you're forfeiting the intangible riches God has to offer, such as joy, grace, kindness, and love.

For example, many people have a house but not a home. Many people have money but not peace. Many people have plans but not a purpose. The essence of life is far more important and valuable than the assets attached to it, because the essence will last longer than life itself (see 1 Cor. 3:11-15).

This principle of saving and losing your life is fixed. It's an if-then clause set in the spiritual laws that govern our existence and eternity. If and when you totally give yourself to God as His kingdom disciple, you're positioned to fully experience the abundant life Christ died to give you both now and forever (see John 10:10).

**What's God calling you to forfeit and lay aside in order to follow Him more completely?**

## Prayer

Loving Heavenly Father, I want to use my time on earth
to live fully as a kingdom disciple. Give me discernment
to choose wisely what will bring You glory and others good.
Help me view my whole life in light of Your kingdom
and Your purposes. I'm Yours. In Christ's name, amen.

# Day 3

# PROCLAIMING CHRIST AND MAKING HIM KNOWN

In Matthew 28:19 Jesus told those gathered around Him in Galilee to make disciples. But He added one stipulation as part of the command: "of all the nations." Thus, the concern of discipleship isn't just for individuals, our own spheres around us, or even our churches but also for systems that affect people's lives, including government and nations.

That was a big task for those gathered around Jesus that day, even though the known world was limited to the Roman Empire. To make disciples of all nations, the early disciples would have to risk their lives covering territory and engaging with cultures that not only opposed them but also sought to harm them. They would need to possess and carry out kingdom authority to accomplish Christ's calling.

Disciples were never sent out only to build a church. While their mission certainly included building the church, it wasn't limited to that. With today's focus on church growth and small groups, we may need to remind ourselves of this critical truth. Christ sent the disciples out to exercise dominion in His name.

That's why the Jewish leaders got angry when the apostles came on the scene (see Acts 4). They couldn't keep these guys quiet. They jailed them and whipped them, but Peter and the others kept preaching and proclaiming the good news of Jesus Christ. Later the Jews in Thessalonica even said, "These men who have upset the world have come here also" (see Acts 17:6).

**What gave the apostles the boldness to stand in the temple and preach right under the noses of the religious leaders who had the authority to flog, imprison, and even execute them?**

**Read Acts 2:1-4. How did the Holy Spirit radically change the disciples' lives?**

**How important is it for believers today to abide in the Holy Spirit's presence and access His power? What are some ways you can do that?**

**Read Acts 9:19-25; 17:5-9. What reactions or occurrences resulted from Paul's effort to proclaim Christ and make disciples?**

**Consider the example of the early church leaders who shared the gospel. How different are our contemporary approaches from theirs?**

When the early believers went about the business of disciple making, they elicited a reaction; people were shaken up. Yet far too often when church people show up today, they find a place where they can relax and be comfortable. Nothing is demanded or expected of them.

Paul, on the other hand, always started something everywhere he went, not because he was a troublemaker but because he preached Jesus. He lived and breathed Jesus and expected others to do the same. He was a disciple, and that's where the trouble started.

Do you realize that Christ has commanded us as His disciples to make an impact on our communities? It's a command. He doesn't want us to be just another resident of our neighborhood or church, failing to make an impact for His kingdom.

When Jesus was on earth, no one was neutral toward Him. People either loved and revered Him or hated and tried to kill Him. But nobody ignored Him.

**What are some ways you could proclaim Jesus and make disciples more intentionally?**

**What are some reservations you have in proclaiming Christ and seeking to make disciples of others?**

**Read Luke 8:14. What light does this verse shed on the reason many believers today don't live as kingdom disciples or don't seek to replicate kingdom disciples?**

**Read Romans 1:16. How does shame prevent believers from making disciples today?**

The world today is largely ignoring Christians and the church on a myriad of issues because it isn't witnessing the authority we speak about, sing about, pray about, and preach about. What's worse is that many Christians aren't interested in Jesus either. Empty religion has replaced relationship. The church desperately needs people who are on fire from the power of the Holy Spirit, who have a burning desire to proclaim and serve Jesus, and who are so excited about Him that they're willing to take the risk of shaking up the status quo to make Him known.

You can't be like Jesus in your job, in your neighborhood, and possibly even in your church without facing opposition. Jesus and all His New Testament followers experienced persecution. You can't expect to escape it. Persecution—whether it comes through rejection, ridicule, or outright tribulation—is part and parcel of being a kingdom disciple. If you're having an easy time in your Christian life or if Satan never bothers you, you may want to check the depth of your discipleship and the authenticity of your obedience to Christ.

**What keeps you from proclaiming Christ as faithfully as you should?**

**Read Mark 4:1-20. Which soil do you most identify with? What needs to change in your life, based on your answer to the first question?**

**What reason has God given you to trust Him beyond your fears? Why should you allow your faith to lead you beyond your comfort zone?**

## Prayer

Dear Lord, I give You permission to develop me as a kingdom disciple in a way that ignites a fire in my soul to proclaim Jesus Christ. Forgive me for neglecting so great a salvation by failing to pursue with passion the calling of making You known both near and far. In Christ's name, amen.

# Day 4
# THE GYMNASIUM
# OF DISCIPLESHIP

Discipleship wasn't a new idea in New Testament times. It was a well-established concept in the Greek world in the centuries before Christ. The word *disciple* means "learner" or "student."

The Greeks had disciples in the realm of philosophy. Plato, who's often referred to as the father of philosophy, developed a system of thought in the realms of epistemology (how we gain knowledge) and the meaning of life. Plato discipled his student Aristotle, who took what he learned and built gymnasiums. In the ancient world, gymnasiums weren't just arenas for sporting events. They were also training centers or academies for teaching students Plato's thought and the system developed by Aristotle, known as Aristotelian logic. The students thus trained were *gymnatized*, the verb form of the Greek word for *gymnasium*.

This discipling process was so successful that it allowed the Greeks to influence the whole Greco-Roman world. Through this process, called Hellenization, people who weren't Greek began to adopt Greek thinking, language, and culture. That was the influence and impact of discipleship.

The New Testament applied this concept in a spiritual context so that we would know what it means to be a disciple of Jesus Christ and to wield the kingdom influence that disciples were intended to have. As in the Greek system, Christian discipleship involves apprenticeship in which the apprentice, or student, is nurtured toward a particular goal.

**Read Matthew 10:24-25 and identify two characteristics of a disciple.**

1.

2.

A disciple is to be like the master, reflecting the master in every way. A disciple is one who is trained and nurtured to be like Jesus Christ.

**Imagine you're learning a new trade from an experienced practitioner, but you choose not to follow your teacher's instruction. What does the refusal to follow instruction demonstrate about your feelings for the teacher?**

**What happens when a disciple of Jesus Christ chooses to ignore His instruction? How does this behavior reflect on Jesus Christ?**

The goal of discipleship is conformity to the Savior, being transformed into the image or likeness of Christ. For example, we know from Scripture that "God is love" (1 John 4:8). Therefore, because Jesus Christ is one in essence and personhood with the Trinity, Jesus is love. So we, as His disciples, ought to reflect a spirit of love to those around us.

Consider what happens when a believer becomes irritated from waiting in a long line and reveals that irritation to everyone around. It may seem like a small thing, but many small things eventually add up to be large things. The highest aim of a kingdom disciple is to replicate Christ's character, conduct, and compassion before the people around us.

**Read the following verses.**

> Those whom He foreknew, He also predestined to become conformed to the image of His Son, so that He would be the firstborn among many brethren.
> Romans 8:29

> The Lord is the Spirit, and where the Spirit of the Lord is, there is liberty. But we all, with unveiled face, beholding as in a mirror the glory of the Lord, are being transformed into the same image from glory to glory, just as from the Lord, the Spirit.
> 2 Corinthians 3:17-18

**What does it mean to become "conformed to the image" of Christ and "transformed into" His image?**

**Describe a person you know who's being conformed to the image of Christ. What makes his or her life distinct?**

**What are one or two areas in your life where you'd like to be more like Jesus? What's one practical step you can take this week to move closer to Jesus in those areas?**

A pastor friend of mine was visiting a college campus a number of years ago. He didn't know that my son Anthony Jr. was a student there. Walking across campus, my friend saw a young man in the distance and then stopped dead in his tracks. *That has to be Tony Evans's son,* he told himself. *He looks like Tony; he's built like Tony; he even walks like Tony.*

He was right, of course. The young man he had spotted was Anthony. Even though the man was a long way off, Anthony's characteristics were so obviously like mine that my friend told me, "I didn't even know Anthony was in college yet. All I knew was that nobody could look that much like you and not be yours."

People ought to be able to see you from a long way off and say, "That person has to be a follower of Jesus Christ." They ought to be able to tell by the way you walk and talk, by the total orientation of your life, that you belong to Christ, because nobody could function the way you function and not know Him.

In other words, the family resemblance ought to be obvious. It ought to be clear where you stand. That's what it means to be a kingdom disciple. You pattern your life after Christ and follow Him so closely that you speak, act, and think like Him and have a passion to help others do the same.

**Take time today to memorize 2 Corinthians 5:17. Use this space to record it and reflect on its meaning.**

**Identify "old things" in your life—thoughts, actions, or attitudes—that have "passed away." In what ways has your relationship with Jesus Christ made you new?**

Being a kingdom disciple means embracing God's will for your life and allowing it to become more important than your own will. You must be able to pray with Jesus:

> Yours is the kingdom and the power
> and the glory forever. Amen.
> MATTHEW 6:13

A kingdom disciple pursues God's kingdom agenda. If that means staying single, you're ready to do that for His sake. If that means staying in a marriage even though you aren't happy in it, you're ready to do that. If that means staying in a job you don't like to which He has called you, you're ready. If that means falling short of all your personal goals because you're striving for His goals instead, that's OK. Doing God's will as His disciple and reflecting His character throughout your days will get you to the place, like Paul, where you can say, "I have finished the course" (2 Tim. 4:7). That's your goal as a kingdom disciple.

**Spend a few moments in silent reflection. Ask God to show you areas where you're choosing your will above His will for your life. What adjustments do you need to make?**

Identify a few periods in your life when you've seen significant spiritual growth. What did God do during those times to transform you, conforming you to His image?

How do we become sensitive to the Holy Spirit's nudging and leading in our lives?

What steps is He leading you to take this week?

## Prayer

Lord, I want to live as a reflection of who You are in all I am. I ask that You'll bring about situations in my life to deepen my relationship with You and help conform me to your image. I love You and want to please You in all I do and in all I am. In Christ's name, amen.

# Day 5

# Go, Baptize, and Teach

As we come to the end of our first week together, I hope you're starting to see how critical discipleship is. It's the key to unlocking the power and authority you need to live as a disciple of Jesus Christ. Not only are we learning that becoming a disciple is our highest calling, but we're also discovering that making disciples goes hand in hand with that calling.

The phrase "make disciples" in Matthew 28:19 is a command in the Greek language of the New Testament; in fact, it's the only command in the Great Commission. The other three activities—going, baptizing, and teaching—are participles that explain and expand the method for making disciples.

We have Jesus' authority and command to make disciples. This means He's with us in the process to ensure that it works when we do it right.

Now that we know what a disciple is, let's take a closer look at Jesus' three-step plan in Matthew 28:19-20 for making disciples.

**What does the word *go* mean in Matthew 28:19?**

**In what ways have you incorporated sharing the good news
of Jesus Christ as you go about your everyday life?**

**In what ways have you intentionally gone to other places to share
the good news of Jesus Christ?**

**GO.** Whether we share the good news of Jesus Christ as we go about our day-to-day lives or travel to another town, community, or country, the command is the same. We're to share the good news of Jesus Christ as a natural outgrowth of our lives, whether near or far. This practice is called evangelism.

*Evangelism* is sharing the good news of Christ's substitutionary death, resurrection, and free offer of forgiveness for sin and eternal life to all who come to Him by faith. Evangelism is done with the clear intent of bringing people to faith in Jesus Christ for salvation. They must be born again into the kingdom before they can develop into disciples of the kingdom.

> **Do you view Jesus' command to evangelize others as something only certain Christians should do or as something every believer is called to do? Explain.**

**BAPTIZE.** After we go, the next part of making disciples is baptizing people who've accepted Christ. The point of baptism isn't merely getting people wet. The point is the public declaration of their identification with Jesus Christ as Lord and Savior.

In fact, the primary meaning of the Greek word for *baptism* is "identification." This was a very picturesque word in New Testament days. It was used of dipping a cloth into a dye so that the cloth became completely identified with the dye by absorbing its color. The cloth was immersed in the dye until it took on the character of the dye. The cloth underwent a complete identity change.

When people put their trust in Christ, they become so completely identified with Him that His death and resurrection to new life become their death and resurrection.

> **Read Romans 6:3-4. What's the result of salvation and the public testimony of that salvation in baptism?**

**TEACH.** The last step in the process of making disciples is teaching others. After people have believed the gospel and have been identified with Christ, we must teach them "to observe all that I commanded you" (Matt. 28:20). Our teaching must start with solid content because Christians are people of the truth and people of the Book. Jesus' commands we're to obey are recorded in the Word.

The goal of biblical teaching is to combine information and knowledge with skill in applying the truth to daily life. After Jesus had taught the people and then fed four thousand (see Mark 8:1-9), He "immediately" had His disciples get into a boat and head out (v. 10).

According to Mark 8:14-21, Jesus wanted the disciples to apply the lesson they had just learned about His power to meet their needs. Jesus asked them some pointed questions about what they had seen and heard in His provision for the crowd, ending with "Do you not yet understand?" (v. 21). Obviously they didn't, but you can be sure they thought about it for a long time, and eventually the message got through.

**Do you need to be a Bible scholar to teach God's Word? Why or why not?**

**What resources are available today to deepen your understanding and application of God's Word so that you can learn it, live it, and teach it (see Ezra 7:10)?**

Making disciples is a process of spiritual development. It's similar to film processing before we had digital cameras. We took a roll of film called negatives to someone to be developed into positives. Our pictures then looked like they were supposed to, accurately reflecting the images we had sought to capture.

Similarly, God wants to take the negatives in our lives into His darkroom and turn them into positives so that we come out looking like His Son. Discipleship is that process by which we're developed into the image of Jesus Christ. And making disciples is our role in helping others experience the same transformation.

## *Prayer*

Dear Heavenly Father, I accept Your command to go, baptize, and teach others to become like You. I want to do this with my life in every way possible. Give me courage when I need it, open doors I can walk through, and insight and understanding of Your Word. In Christ's name, amen.

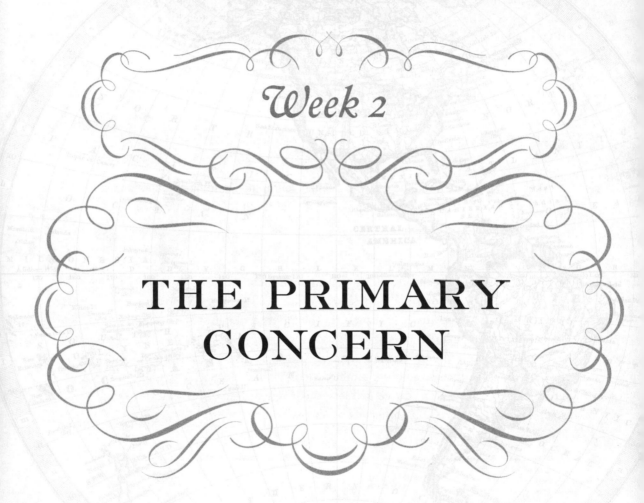

Week 2

# THE PRIMARY CONCERN

*Group Experience*

# START

*Welcome to session 2 of* Kingdom Disciples.

**What was a helpful point of review or a new insight gained from your personal study last week?**

**Does anybody have any stories or updates related to our discussion and application from the previous group session?**

This week we'll turn our attention to the primary concern of a kingdom disciple.

**What's the best fictional book you've ever read? How would you describe the main subject of this book?**

People learn to read early in their education. Reading forms a foundation that allows us to interact with many other disciplines; it's foundational. As we work our way through school, we move from the basics of reading to reading comprehension. One key to understanding what you read is the ability to identity the main point of the book. Like every other good book, the Bible has a primary concern. The primary concern of the Bible—from Genesis to Revelation—is the glory of God through the advancement of His kingdom.

Before we learn what Dr. Evans has to teach us about making the kingdom of God our primary concern, would somebody pray for our time together, asking the Lord to open our hearts and minds to His Word as we begin this study?

 # WATCH

*Refer to this view guide as you watch video session 2.*

### KINGDOM DISCIPLE

A Christian who is progressively participating in the process of learning what it is to live all of life under the lordship, rulership, kingship of Jesus Christ

The primary concern that you should have as a kingdom disciple is to seek ye first the kingdom.

From Genesis to Revelation, the one subject of the Bible is the glory of God through the advancement of His kingdom.

The church would be the new mechanism through which God would express His kingdom rule in history until such time He renewed it with His people Israel.

You and I are God's official representatives to represent His presence, His person, and His authority in history.

Righteousness is the standards by which the kingdom operates, the rules by which the kingdom works.

There are two answers to every question—God's answer and everybody else's—and everybody else is wrong when they disagree with God.

God must be first in your priorities; first in your passions; and most important, first in your decisions.

Only as a kingdom disciple—a visible, verbal, full-time representative of Jesus Christ—can you expect to receive all that God has determined for you to have, because you're operating under His rule.

God says, "If you operate in My kingdom, under My rule, according to My standards, I will cover you because you put Me first."

 # DISCUSS

*Discuss the video with your group, using these questions.*

What did Dr. Evans say is the one subject of the Bible? Where else in Scripture do we see this subject reflected?

If God's rule is the master key to the kingdom, what are we unable to access if we don't take hold of this key?

The church is God's plan to assert His kingdom rule in the world. How is this group contributing to this mission?

Dr. Evans said, "You and I are living in a day when the rules are changing at warp speed." Why should we continue to seek God first when our culture is dismissing His standard of righteousness?

What happens when we choose the rules of this world instead of the standards that emanate from God?

The key word in Matthew 6:33 is *first*. Why is it so tempting for us to make God second in our priorities? Who or what do you elevate to the level of first priority?

Jesus said that once God is first, all other things will be added to you. How does placing God first allow us to see everything else in our lives clearly?

Ask someone to read Matthew 6:25-34. Why does worry creep into our lives when we don't make God and His kingdom our primary concern? What concerns are you experiencing that would go away if you sought God's kingdom above everything else?

Dr. Evans stated that when he was young, though his family didn't have a lot, he didn't worry because he knew his daddy would provide. Most of the time when we make something other than God a priority, it's because we feel that God won't give us something we need. What are you afraid to trust God to provide?

*Read week 2 and complete the activities before the next group session.*

# KINGDOM CONCERNS

As we continue our journey through the depths, clefts, and mountaintops that make up God's kingdom, let's broaden our road map by looking more deeply at this overarching concept of God's kingdom. The Greek word the Bible uses for *kingdom* means "rule" or "authority." Thus, when we talk about a kingdom, we're talking first about a king or a ruler. We're talking about someone who's in charge.

If there's a ruler, there also have to be "rulees," or kingdom subjects. In addition, a kingdom includes a realm—a domain over which the king rules. Finally, if there are a ruler, rulees, and a realm, there also have to be kingdom regulations—guidelines that govern the relationship between the ruler and the subjects. These are necessary so that the rulees will know whether they're doing what the ruler wants them to do.

God's kingdom includes all of these elements. He's the absolute Ruler of His domain, which encompasses all of creation. Everything God rules, He runs—even when it doesn't look as if He's running it. Even when life looks as if it's out of control, God is running its out-of-controlness.

God's kingdom also has rulees. Colossians 1:13 says everybody who has trusted the Lord Jesus Christ as Savior has been transferred from the kingdom of darkness to the kingdom of light. If you're a believer in Jesus Christ, your allegiance has changed. You no longer align yourself with Satan but with Christ. This week let's look at what your primary concern ought to be as Christ's kingdom disciple.

## *Day 1*

# FIRST THINGS FIRST

As we begin our second week of study together, let's refresh our minds on what a kingdom disciple is. A kingdom disciple is a believer who participates in the spiritual-development process of progressively learning to live all of life under the lordship of Jesus Christ. To live all of life under Christ assumes that you know and apply what Christ desires for you to do in life.

**Read Matthew 6:33. What should our primary concern be as a kingdom disciple?**

**How do we "seek first His kingdom" in everyday, practical terms?**

**What would change about the way you make decisions if seeking first the kingdom and God's righteousness became the primary concern of your life?**

**When is a time you sought God's kingdom, His perspective, and His desires first in your life and experienced deliverance, provision, or peace as a result? What did you learn from this experience?**

To live life to its fullest and to accomplish and experience all God has created you to do, you must place God and His kingdom first. God's rule isn't to be one among many. God can't be second; He must be first. The problem for most of us is that God is merely in the vicinity of our lives; He isn't first in our lives.

I often hear people tell me they just don't have enough time for God. What they're really telling me is God isn't in first place in their lives, because people always make time for what matters most. Recall a time when you were dating someone you deeply loved. Love was new, and you couldn't get that person off your mind. The number of hours in your day didn't increase, and the number of minutes in an hour didn't increase. And yet for some reason you were able to find the time necessary to show your dedication and devotion to the person you loved.

We always have enough time for what we prioritize in our lives. Lack of discipleship isn't caused by a lack of time. Lack of discipleship is caused by a failure to prioritize our time.

Not seeking the kingdom as our primary concern has led to a diminishing experience of God. Yet the rule, blessings, guidance, and provisions of heaven can be fully realized only as God's kingdom standards are prioritized by His disciples. God has made it perfectly clear throughout Scripture that His rightful place in our lives is first.

**Read Proverbs 3:9. What priority do you give God in your finances?**

**Read Revelation 2:4. What did Jesus say the church had done? What causes us to consider other loves more valuable than Jesus?**

**Read Colossians 1:18. Christ is to have what place over what?**

Jesus Christ is to have first place over everything, including our thoughts, actions, decisions, time, and talents. This is His rightful place in our lives. Not only that, but Jesus said we're to seek first God and His kingdom above all else. A kingdom disciple does nothing less than that.

When you don't revere God as the supreme Ruler, His kingdom and its benefits aren't yours. Matthew 6:33 states that when you put God and His kingdom rule first, then "all these things" will be given to you. All what things? Everything you need and everything that's necessary for you to fully live out your destiny and purpose.

That doesn't mean you won't have problems or challenges in life. It means you'll be well equipped to overcome or persevere through those problems and challenges when all of life is aligned under God's authority and His rule. A corollary to this principle is that when you don't put God first, you miss out on all of the benefits and blessings of the King and His kingdom.

**When a struggle or challenge arises, where's the first place you look for help? What does this choice communicate about your dependence on God?**

**Why is it important to trust God first with your struggles and challenges?**

**What do we miss in our relationship with the Lord when we try to solve our problems without consulting Him?**

If you're a parent, maybe you recall saying these words to your children: "Why didn't you talk to me first? I wish you would talk to me first." Often parents point out that their children could have avoided mistakes or problems in life if they had simply sought and followed their advice as parents first. While this principle holds true in parenting, it holds even more true with God. Many people wonder why they aren't hearing from God or experiencing His abiding presence and victory in their lives. God's answer to their question is simply "Because you come to Me last. In fact, you first go to the world—a system that leaves Me out. And then you come to Me only when the world's advice doesn't help."

The key to success as a kingdom disciple is found in the word *first*. It's in the prioritization of the rule of God over every area of life where the power for kingdom living is found.

**What action communicate that God is first in our lives?**

**How do spiritual disciplines like Bible study and prayer create dependency and on God and priority in our relationship with Him?**

## *Prayer*

Loving Heavenly Father, give me a heart that instinctively places You first. Ignite a passion in my soul to seek You above all else. Draw near to me as I draw near to You so that I can discern Your presence, guidance, and power working in and through me. Show me the value of putting You first as I commit myself to You as Your disciple. In Christ's name, amen.

## *Day 2*
# WORRY NO LONGER

One day a man was rushing to catch his plane at the airport because he was late. Worried that he might miss his flight, he started weaving in and out of the crowds of people walking to their gates with moves that would make an NFL running back proud. He bumped into a man dressed in a flight uniform and briefly paused to say he was sorry. The man asked him why he was rushing, and he told him that he was trying to catch his flight. "Where are you going?" the man in the flight uniform asked.

"I'm going to Austin," he replied.

"Well, then, relax and stop worrying," the man said with a smile. "I'm the pilot, and that plane won't go anywhere without me."

Immediately the man who had been running through the airport worried about missing his flight was able to slow down and rest because he knew where the pilot was. Similarly, knowing where God is located—knowing what He promises when you look to Him first—will reduce your anxiety, frustration, and irritation on all levels.

In Matthew 6:33 Jesus told us that when we put God first as His kingdom disciple, He will take care of everything else. That truth alone ought to be enough motivation to obey this command.

**The context of Matthew 6:33 reveals a lot about the benefits of its promise. Identify the common word that's used in the following verses.**

**Matthew 6:25**

**Matthew 6:27**

**Matthew 6:28**

**Matthew 6:31**

**Matthew 6:34**

**How can first seeking God alleviate worry in a person's life?**

**In what way does faith affect the amount of worry a person experiences?**

In yesterday's lesson we looked at the importance of putting God first in our thoughts, actions, and lives. We considered God's desire for us to place Him first and examined His rightful place in our lives. Today I want to show you a direct benefit that will come to you when you choose to place Him first:

> Seeking God and His kingdom first will drastically reduce
> your worry.

You ought to put God's kingdom first if for no other reason than to reduce your personal anxiety and worry. Worry is a common issue plaguing many people today. More than forty million adults in the United States suffer from a diagnosed form of anxiety. Countless millions more no doubt suffer from worry or anxiety on less severe levels. Whether it's worrying about jobs, safety, health, relationships, income, terrorism, or the future, worry rots many people's ability to enjoy the gift of life that God has given them.

**List some of the subjects or circumstances you regularly worry about.**

**In what way can putting God first in your priorities, thoughts, and actions reduce your worry about these things?**

Although Scripture never calls worry a sin, we can infer God's disapproval from the more than seventy commands by Jesus, as well as Old Testament verses instructing us not to fear or worry. In what situations could worrying be considered a sin? Are there situations in which worry wouldn't be a sin?

Read 1 Peter 5:6-11. What four things will God do for you when you replace worry and anxiety with confidence in Him?

1.

2.

3.

4.

The next step in your study of kingdom discipleship is to examine your personal views on seeking God first and the resultant benefits for you.

Read John 3:30. What's your initial reaction to the principle in this verse?

According to Matthew 22:37, in what ways are you to love God? How are those forms of love evident in your life?

Read Psalm 55:22; 56:3; Proverbs 3:5-6; and Philippians 4:6-7. Describe the connections among trust, surrender, and worry.

Are you comfortable with the level of worry in your life? If not, what steps will you take in order to trust, surrender to, and seek God more fully?

Of all the problems you face and the challenges that keep you in perpetual defeat, in which of those problems have you placed God first?

Have you intentionally tried to honor God first in your heart, attitude, choices, and thoughts? How are you seeking His wisdom and will for responding to each situation?

When you seek God first, you can rest because God's got it, and He promises that all these things are already yours in Him.

## Prayer

Jesus, forgive me for worrying and feeling anxious rather than casting my cares on You and turning to You first in prayer and faith. You have everything figured out and in control. All You ask of me is that I put Your will first in my life. Show me how I can embrace a life of true surrender and peace in my daily life. In Christ's name, amen.

*Day 3*

# WHAT GOD CAN'T DO

People are usually surprised when I bring up the subject of certain things God can't do. They look at me with shock as if I just flew over the cuckoo's nest. But God has said there are certain things He can't do. For example:

> … so that by two unchangeable things
> in which it is impossible for God to lie …
> HEBREWS 6:18

> God is not a man, that He should lie,
> Nor a son of man, that He should repent.
> NUMBERS 23:19

> I, the LORD, do not change.
> MALACHI 3:6

> My covenant I will not violate,
> Nor will I alter the utterance of My lips.
> PSALM 89:34

In fact, there are several things God can't do. While Jesus bore our sins on the cross, He didn't sin Himself. This is because God is holy and can't sin. He's perfect in all of His ways.

Do you want to know something else God can't do? God can't be second. He must be first.

**Read Exodus 20:3. What are the implications of this verse?**

**Identify three areas of your life in which God should be first.**

**1.**

**2.**

**3.**

**Is God currently first in those areas? What would need to change for Him to be first?**

In baseball if you miss first base, it doesn't matter whatever else you do. If you run past first base without touching it, touching second, third, or home plate doesn't count. It doesn't matter if everyone in the stands is cheering you or congratulating you when you cross home. If you miss first base, nothing after that matters.

In living as a kingdom disciple, if you fail to seek God's kingdom and His righteousness first, all else is worthless. God has established His rightful place as first. Without surrendering everything to Him, you're on your own.

**Read Romans 12:1-2. Briefly describe the major principles of these two verses in your own words.**

**Verse 1:**

**Verse 2:**

**According to Romans 12:2, God's will has three distinct attributes: good, pleasing, and perfect. Why is sacrifice required for living in this will?**

Truly living out God's good, pleasing, and perfect will begins with personal sacrifice. Throughout Scripture we read that anytime God wanted to do something significant for His people, He always required a sacrifice first. An action had to be taken to demonstrate sincerity and commitment.

Worship isn't simply singing songs on Sunday. True worship, as outlined in Romans 12, is giving yourself to God in your entirety. True worship is total surrender.

I like the story of the chicken and the pig. Both were walking down the street one day when they came to a grocery store with a sign in the window that read, Bacon and Eggs Desperately Needed. The chicken looked at the pig and said, "I'll give them the eggs if you'll give them the bacon."

The pig stared back at the chicken and replied, "No way."

The chicken asked, "Why not?"

The pig replied, "Because for you, it's a contribution; for me, it's my life."

**What did Paul mean when he said we're to be living sacrifices?**

**Read Galatians 2:20. How can a person be crucified with Christ yet alive to God?**

**How often are we called to be a living sacrifice or crucified with Christ throughout the day, week, month, or year?**

Surrendering is more than simply yielding. Sacrificing occurs more than simply on Sunday morning. Both surrender and sacrifice mean committing all of your energy, emotions, thoughts, and actions to God, under His rule and in line with His commands and instructions for your life. Putting God first is an attitude that shows up in everything and everywhere because God's kingdom rules over everything and rules everywhere.

What would happen if you chose to obey the speed limit only in the town where you lived but opted not to when you drove elsewhere? You would get a ticket, and you might also cause an accident. The rule of the United States governs the entire country. Yet far too many Christians today live as if God's rule applies only to certain moments or situations. And then they wonder why they aren't fully experiencing the manifestation of God's authority, power, provision, and blessing in their lives and why they continue to have accidents and mistakes instead.

Living as a kingdom disciple has to take place twenty-four hours a day, seven days a week. It's to be a mindset and a lifestyle, not merely a hobby or a habit you engage in from time to time.

**This week is all about priorities. Make a list of your priorities for this week in the space below.**

**How can you place God first while you're accomplishing these priorities?**

**Do any of these priorities need to change in light of today's study? If so, why?**

## Prayer

Lord and Savior, open my eyes to discover where
I'm failing to put You first in my thoughts, words,
actions, and decisions. Help me set priorities in such
a way that surrender to You becomes natural. Give me
passion to study Your Word, learn Your precepts,
and apply them to my life. In Christ's name, amen.

# Day 4

# Relationship or Religion

An assignment I had in seminary involved writing a research paper. When I turned it in, I was very proud of the work I had put into it. I had done my due diligence. I had controlled the material and made valid arguments. I felt that my paper was strong.

My professor felt otherwise. I could tell by the big zero he wrote in red at the top of the first page. Down at the bottom he had scribbled, "Tony, great work. Great preparation. Wrong assignment."

In my zeal to do this paper well, I had gone off and researched the wrong topic altogether. Yes, I deserved that zero.

Living as a kingdom disciple can be somewhat similar to this experience. It's not that there aren't a lot of people doing a lot of excellent things. It's not that a lot of these same people don't attend church, help the hurting, or say all the correct spiritual phrases. It's just that they've missed the relational connection that comes through voluntary surrender and intentional connection with God. They haven't made Him first in their hearts. They've swapped a relationship with the true, living God with religion and religious practices.

Just as my paper got a zero, religion without relationship won't count for much either when all is said and done.

**Read Matthew 23:13-15. In what way can someone make a proselyte while shutting the door of the kingdom of heaven in his face? Name some ways that can happen in today's contemporary religious culture as well.**

**Read Matthew 23:27. What issue caused Jesus to condemn the Pharisees' practice of religion?**

When have you caught yourself focusing more on religious activities than on your relationship with Jesus? Describe your experience.

Contrast the relationship Jesus described in John 15:1-10 with what you just read in Matthew 23:13-15. What's the difference between obeying God because you love Him and obeying Him in order to earn approval? Which phrase more closely describes your relationship with Jesus?

In what ways do you need to shift your thinking from a list of things to do toward the high calling of a relationship? Take a moment to pray and let Jesus know you want to know Him more fully and to reflect His love in your heart, thoughts, and actions.

External observances—the rules and rituals of religion—can get in the way of a relationship with God. In contrast, when you're motivated by a relationship, surrender comes naturally. God wants to be first in your life as your King, but He wants His relationship with you to be the motivating factor for you as His kingdom disciple. Otherwise, you're simply crossing off a list called religion and therefore failing to access the strength, peace, and power that come by way of His love.

We serve a mighty God who's all-powerful, but never forget that He's closer than you think. When Jesus asked the disciples to abide in Him, it was another way of saying, "Stick with Me." He was inviting them (and us) into a relationship in which they would be cared for and loved. His love is to be your driving passion in putting Him first. God doesn't want you to serve Him only because you're supposed to; He wants you to serve Him because you love Him. Abiding is an invitation to dependence. He wants your morality, prayer life, dedication, and service predicated on your relationship with Him rather than on religious duty. Instead of being defined by what you do, God wants you to be defined by whom you know and whom you represent—Jesus Christ.

**In what ways are you defined by others, by yourself, or by what you do? Consider ways you try to gain significance or purpose through religious activities, whether personal or corporate.**

**In what ways are you defined by who you are in Jesus Christ? Consider how often you align your thoughts about yourself with His truth about who you are and how often you go to Him in conversation or thoughts to experience peace, joy, and love.**

The solution to the challenges of living as a kingdom disciple isn't down here on earth. The beginning point of our identity, as well as the foundation of living as a kingdom disciple, is found in our spiritual relationship with God through His Son, Jesus Christ, and in the abiding presence of the Holy Spirit. One way we can live a life predicated on relationship rather than on religious activity is found in Colossians 3:1:

> If you have been raised up with Christ,
> keep seeking the things above, where Christ
> is, seated at the right hand of God.
> COLOSSIANS 3:1

How do you seek things above? You seek things above with all that's in you. Just as you tell the person you're in love with that you love him or her with all your heart, God wants to have all of our hearts in our relationship with Him. He wants us to set our hearts on things above, where His rule and perspective reign preeminent.

**Read Matthew 16:21-28. When Peter rebuked Jesus for talking about going to Jerusalem and suffering, in what sense did Peter fail to set his heart on things above?**

**Rewrite in your own words Jesus' response to Peter in verse 23.**

**What does setting your mind "on God's interests" mean for living life as a kingdom disciple?**

Discipleship is costly. Living as a true kingdom disciple will cost you something (see vv. 24-25). But that cost will become easier to bear when you're motivated by a deep trust and an abiding relationship with the Lord who loves you enough that He died to redeem you. Only by linking your heart with Christ's heart and your mind with His mind in the heavenlies will you discover the joy, peace, and purpose that come through true surrender.

**Relationships are cultivated through communication. Take additional time today to speak to and hear from God in prayer.**

## *Prayer*

Dear Lord, I choose to let go of the religious activities that distract me from a deep, abiding relationship and fellowship with You. Forgive me for trusting in a list of things to do rather than surrendering my all to You. In Christ's name, amen.

# *Day 5*
# KINGDOM VISION

I'll never forget one not-so-great experience in the shower. It started when I got soap in my eye. As you can imagine, my eye started burning. So I did what comes naturally: I rubbed it. The problem was that I also had soap on my hands, so not only did I fail to get the soap out of my eye, but I also managed to get more soap in both eyes. Now instead of one eye that couldn't see, I had two.

With both eyes closed, I instinctively reached for the towel. As I groped around for the towel in my blindness, I stepped on the bar of soap I had dropped and went flying, hurting both my head and my back. I was left flailing around in the shower with a headache, a backache, and stinging eyes, all because something had blinded me.

Physical blindness, even temporary, can cause a lot of problems. But spiritual blindness is worse. When you're spiritually blind, you'll wind up with more than just a headache and a backache; you'll wind up with a life ache because you can't live successfully in the physical realm if you can't see the spiritual realm, which affects everything else in life.

God's kingdom operates from the realm of heaven, as we discussed in regard to our need to set our hearts on things above. Thus, the only way you'll be able to see life with clear vision is when you view all of life from a heavenly, kingdom perspective.

Jesus said in Matthew 6:22-23 that if you aren't clear about the kingdom—the things of God—you can't see because you're spiritually blind. And if you're spiritually blind, your feet won't know which way to go. Spiritual blindness affects not only your eyes but also all of your life choices.

**Have you had an experience when you had difficulty seeing? Describe some of the challenges you faced.**

**In what ways can failing to prioritize the King and His kingdom cause spiritual blindness in a person's life?**

One result of prioritizing God first is that you get to experience the manifestation of His glory. Romans 11:36 says:

> From Him and through Him and to Him are
> all things. To Him be the glory forever. Amen.
> ROMANS 11:36

As you may already know, *amen* means "So be it." By closing the verse with *amen*, Paul was emphasizing that God's glory is the bottom line in His kingdom. Paul said everything is *from* God. He's the first cause, the source. Then Paul said *through* God, everything is. He's the effective cause of everything in creation. And finally, Paul said everything is *to* Him. He's the final cause. It all returns to Him to bring Him glory forever.

It's crucial to understand that God created the universe for His pleasure and His glory (see Rev. 4:11), including each one of us (see Isa. 43:7). God didn't make the world first and foremost for us but rather for Himself.

Everything is created to bring glory to God. We participate in bringing Him glory by putting Him first in our thoughts, choices, and actions.

*Glory* is a sweet word. It comes from a Greek word that means "to be heavy" or "to have weight." Giving God glory is acknowledging His significance. That's what glory is.

**Read 1 Corinthians 10:31. How does everything we do present an opportunity to glorify God?**

**Does glory come only through the seemingly major things we do, like going on a mission trip or volunteering at a homeless shelter? Why or why not?**

**How do we glorify God in the seemingly ordinary things we do day in and day out?**

**Are there practices or priorities in your life that need to be adjusted so that you can intentionally bring greater glory to God? Consider your speech patterns, use of time, finances, prayer life, and so on.**

Most insurance policies call a natural disaster an act of God. If a storm blows your roof off, for example, that's an act of God. If a hurricane floods a city or a neighborhood, that's an act of God. This type of language assigns blame to God for life's trials.

Yet rarely are we so quick to give God glory when He guides us through a natural disaster with the roof on or the city and neighborhood intact. In all things we ought to give Him glory because He makes it possible for us to eat every day.

Many people run to church when something goes wrong. But people who live as kingdom disciples understand the fullness of God's power and the preeminence of His position over all, so they come into His presence to give Him glory no matter what. Living for God's glory means saying, "Lord, my goal today is to reflect Your significance. I want to ascribe to You the glory that already belongs to You. I want to radiate, demonstrate, magnify, and illustrate Your glory." That's a life lived as a true kingdom disciple.

**Take some time to memorize Romans 11:36. Record it as you contemplate God's greatness, sovereignty, and power.**

**We don't typically have idols like the ones in Old Testament times. But what are some things in our contemporary culture that usurp God's glory in our lives?**

**Turn your attention to your own heart. What idols are blinding you from seeing God's glory?**

One of the first toys I played with as a young boy growing up in Baltimore was a little jack-in-the-box clown that popped up to the tune "Pop Goes the Weasel." I loved that toy. And while that concept is great for a toy, it isn't so great for God.

Yet that's how many people try to treat God—a clown in a box who pops up whenever we want Him to appear and do our bidding: "Bless me now, Lord. I'm turning the handle. Come on, pop up." Then we stuff Him back down in the box and close the top when we don't want to see Him anymore or when we don't want to be burdened by His demands.

A kingdom disciple, however, lives by these words:

> Not My will, but Yours be done.
> LUKE 22:42

> ... on earth as it is in heaven.
> MATTHEW 6:10

In Matthew 13:11 Jesus said the kingdom is a mystery to those who aren't willing to hear, see, and understand what God is doing. But it's a grand adventure for those who are willing to acknowledge God in His rightful place as first over all.

One of the easiest ways to identify personal idols is by looking at ways you spend your time and your money. Think back over the past month. Where did your money go? Where was your time spent?

What are some ways you can more closely align your schedule and your budget to reflect God's rightful priority in your heart and mind?

## Prayer

Loving Lord and Savior, I seek first You and Your righteousness. I want You to rule over my thoughts, words, and actions. Your ways are higher than my ways, and Your thoughts are higher than my thoughts. Let me live all of my life under Your comprehensive rule so that I can give You the glory and the praise that are due Your name, all the while experiencing the power and blessings You've promised in Your Word. In Christ's name, amen.

KINGDOM DISCIPLES

Week 3

# THE BOLD CONFESSION

*Group Experience*

# START

*Welcome to session 3 of* Kingdom Disciples.

**What was a helpful point of review or a new insight gained from your personal study last week?**

**Does anybody have any stories or updates related to our discussion and application from the previous group session?**

This week we'll look at what it means to be a confessing kingdom disciple.

**What's your favorite sports team? How long have you followed it?**

**What are some ways we let people know what team we like?**

People talk about the things they enjoy. Fans of a sport team have no problem entering conversations about their favorite sports, players, or teams. We know scores and statistics. We memorialize key plays or games. Being a fan is an identification we're glad to take on ourselves because it costs us very little. But can we say the same about our identification with Christ? How many people know we're followers of Jesus? Are we verbal, visible followers of Jesus? Today Dr. Evans will talk about what it means to confess Christ with our lives.

Before we learn what Dr. Evans has to teach us on the confession of a kingdom disciple, would somebody pray for our time together, asking the Lord to open our hearts and minds to His Word?

#  WATCH

*Refer to this viewer guide as you watch video session 3.*

A person is saved for eternity by faith alone in Christ alone.

When the Bible talks about discipleship, it talks about a cost.

You're saved by faith apart from works (Rom. 4), but you become a disciple by a faith that does work (Jas. 2).

Faith without work will keep your faith dormant. Your Christianity won't work for you.

The word *saved,* when you're not saved, means to be delivered from eternal separation from God. When you are saved, it means God delivering you in history.

Discipleship requires a commitment.

## THE COMMITMENT TO BE A DISCIPLE

1. Come to Him.  2. Carry your cross.

Your cross, as a kingdom disciple, is the price tag that comes with your public identification with Him.

To be a kingdom disciple means that you wisely, lovingly, and appropriately make it clear that you are a Christian.

It is your willingness to be connected with Jesus that makes you a disciple.

## THREE TENSES OF SALVATION

1. Salvation past from the penalty of sin—being born again

2. Salvation future from the presence of sin—glorification

3. Salvation from the power of sin—sanctification

Confession is related to your deliverance in history, not your deliverance in eternity.

You are not only a Christian going to heaven. You're a kingdom disciple who has heaven joining you on earth.

# DISCUSS

*Discuss the video with your group, using these questions.*

Dr. Evans began by talking about the difference between taking a class for credit and auditing a class because you're interested in the subject matter. What's the difference between being a disciple and someone who merely audits the Christian life?

Compare Romans 4:3-5 and James 2:14-17. How do these passages complement each other? What essential aspects of the Christian faith does each one teach?

Salvation is free, but discipleship requires a commitment. What has it cost you to follow Jesus?

Read Luke 14:26-27. What two specific costs of discipleship can be identified from these verses? What did Jesus mean when He said a disciple must "hate his own father and mother and wife and children and brothers and sisters" (v. 26)?

Dr. Evans pointed out that Jesus' public display of carrying the cross shifted sentiment about Him. As we begin to follow Jesus, what might change about the way our culture views us?

What's your cross to carry?

We live in a society that's growing more pluralistic by the day. Many are tempted to hide their belief in Jesus. Why is speaking about Jesus necessary for a Christian (see Acts 4:18-20)?

Read Romans 10:9-10. Based on Dr. Evans's teaching, how should we understand confession in the context of these verses?

Why must Christians be both visible and verbal followers of Jesus?

*Read week 3 and complete the activities before the next group session.*

# KINGDOM CONFESSION

If you were accused of being a Christian on your job or in your community, would there be enough evidence to convict you? Or would you be found innocent?

Jesus made a clear connection between His followers' public acknowledgment and confession of Him before people and His confession of us before the Father. Jesus didn't say if you confess His Father before people, He would confess you before Him. Confessing that you believe in God wasn't His goal. After all, it's easy to say you believe in God. People pour so many variant definitions into the word *God* that just saying the name doesn't always convey a degree of commitment.

However, when you publicly confess Jesus Christ, everyone knows whom you're talking about. The name Jesus can't be confused or watered down.

Publicly confessing Jesus can be compared to a married person who wears a wedding ring. That wedding ring is on the ring finger to make a public declaration of a legal, binding relationship with someone else. You can be married and choose not to wear your ring so that no one will know you're married, but I doubt that your spouse will condone that choice.

A lot of Christians today who've married into the family of God as the bride of Jesus Christ don't want to wear His ring. They don't want other people to know they're bound to Jesus in a covenant relationship. When it's not convenient to be associated with Jesus, they simply say, like Peter, "I don't know the man." Jesus made it clear that because of this choice, when they call on Him and He's acting as the mediator between them and God the Father, He will deny that He knows them.

This week we're going to look at the ways your private commitment to Jesus and your public confession of Him affect the level of His power and authority that you experience in your life. Few people realize the connection between committing to and confessing Jesus and overcoming life's challenges. But when you make that connection and live it out, you're on your way to fully realizing all you were created to be and do as a kingdom disciple.

# *Day 1*
# FOXES HAVE HOLES

Foxes are interesting creatures. Their small frames and bushy tales offer a deceptive appearance of gentleness. Yet foxes are anything but gentle. With a stealthlike hunting ability, they often pounce on their prey from seemingly nowhere, thus obliterating any chances it has for survival in just a manner of seconds.

Foxes don't discriminate when it comes to what to have for breakfast, lunch, or dinner. Any small mammal will do. In addition to taking the lives of these mammals, foxes sometimes take their dens. Foxes have been known to overtake the living quarters of rabbits, badgers, and other mammals in their efforts to find a warm, safe environment for sleeping.

Foxes set the scene as we consider a kingdom disciple's commitment to Jesus Christ. After all, it was Jesus who made the comparison between foxes and Himself when He said:

> The foxes have holes and the birds of the air have nests,
> but the Son of Man has nowhere to lay His head.
> MATTHEW 8:20

When a man asked Jesus if he could follow Him, Jesus expressed a spiritual principle by using a physical, tangible illustration. That principle is the unpredictable, uncertain, and often physically limiting realities that can surround a disciple. While foxes may have dens they've swiped from a rabbit or a badger to sleep in, Jesus made it clear that if we want to follow Him, we aren't guaranteed even that much comfort.

**Based on your knowledge of Scripture and the life of Christ, list three other common provisions or predictable patterns in life that Jesus lacked while on earth.**

1.

2.

3.

**A disciple is to imitate the master. What comforts or certainties in life would you be willing to forfeit if Jesus asked you to do so? Why or why not? What would be the challenges you would face in doing so?**

**What's a positive outcome of sacrificing physical needs or wants for a greater calling?**

Jesus explained to His audience that if they weren't willing to endure physical privation in order to follow Him or if they were going to prioritize their family, security, or way of life over Him (see Matt. 8:21-22; Luke 9:61-62), they weren't fit for His kingdom.

Simply put, looking back to what you know, feel comfortable with, or rely on after starting out on the path of discipleship doesn't cut it. Why is that? Just as a farmer can't plow a straight line while looking over his shoulder, you can't move forward in your faith accurately and authoritatively with your eyes set on anything but Jesus Himself.

Jesus was saying that if you try to plow looking back, you can't carry out His kingdom agenda. Do you remember Lot's wife? She had left Sodom, but Sodom hadn't left her. Although she had been put under a mandatory evacuation plan by God Himself, she didn't want to leave her comfort zone, history, or possessions. As she started to leave town, she began to regret leaving. She looked back despite the angel's warning (see Gen. 19:17), and God stopped her right there (see v. 26). Unable to evacuate or return, she lost everything—even her life.

**Read Genesis 22:1-12. How did Abraham's obedience to God differ from that of Lot's wife? Was Lot's wife's partial obedience true obedience? Explain.**

**Have you ever shrunk from obeying God in an area in which you knew He was asking you for full commitment? How was God's work in your life affected?**

**Read Matthew 22:37. What word appears repeatedly? Define it.**

When you choose to live as a kingdom disciple, Jesus doesn't guarantee a roof over your head, a promotion at work, or social popularity. Being a kingdom disciple isn't a sure way to success as the world defines it. Every disciple other than John died for his faith.

Read that sentence again. Every disciple other than John died for his faith. Underline it. Meditate on it. Don't skip over it, considering it buried in the dusty annals of church history. "Jesus Christ is the same yesterday and today and forever" (Heb. 13:8). His call to discipleship is no easier now than it was when He walked on earth. His first fully committed kingdom disciples didn't die a peaceful death, at a ripe old age, surrounded by family and friends. Most of them died brutal deaths. Some were even crucified upside down.

**Read the following verses and record similarities in what they say about the cost of discipleship: Mark 8:34; Luke 14:27; John 15:18; Philippians 1:21; 2:5-8.**

Before we go further in this study, are you sure you want to be a committed kingdom disciple? This isn't a fast-track ticket to the top. If you commit to truly being a kingdom disciple, there will be a cost. That's guaranteed.

Few people are willing to pay those costs today. That's why we have so few kingdom disciples. And that's also why believers are experiencing so little power, authority, and victory in our own lives and are having so little impact on the lives of others.

People embrace comfort today. Kingdom disciples are often called to forgo comfort for the cause of Christ. How is a willingness to set aside your comfort a confession that you're willing to live for Jesus?

What are some comforts you enjoy that God may be calling you to let go of to pursue Christ more fully?

How does being supported by a community of kingdom disciples help you persevere in your confession, even when it becomes costly and difficult?

## Prayer

Loving Lord, being Your kingdom disciple isn't a stroll down easy street. It comes with a high cost of committing to You, Your plan, Your way, and Your will. I admit that can be scary to think about. Give me the courage I need to live as Your disciple so that I can fully experience Your presence in my life. In Christ's name, amen.

## Day 2

# Nails, Wood, Doors and Roofing

Have you ever built a new home, or have you ever hired a builder to construct one for you? If you have, then you know that before the grader ever hits the ground to clear the way for the foundation, the finances must be discussed. No new-home builder sets out to construct a house without verifying the buyer's financial viability and credibility. He also calculates an estimate of expected costs so that by the time the house is built, there's little doubt that the buyer can afford it.

We've been doing a major renovation job on a quaint, large home built in the 1930s. When it's done, the refurbished facility will serve as our Tony Evans Training Center's media hub for recording Bible studies and creating online courses. Before we set out to start the project, we sat down with the builder to look at anticipated costs. Yet, as you may know if you've built or refurbished a home yourself, some changes came later on that we hadn't known about at the start. For example, we needed a bit more soundproofing so that vehicle and airplane noise wouldn't hinder the filming that would take place. The new expenses required a change order that tacked on the new cost, thus keeping a documented financial trail for the entire project.

If these change orders hadn't been discussed or if we had proceeded with the initial financial assumptions, it's possible that when the building was done, we wouldn't have had the needed funds to pay the contractors.

Counting the cost is what Jesus was referring to when He compared the commitment of discipleship to building a new home:

> Which one of you, when he wants to build a tower, does not first sit down and calculate the cost to see if he has enough to complete it? Otherwise, when he has laid a foundation and is not able to finish, all who observe it begin to ridicule him, saying, "This man began to build and was not able to finish."
> Luke 14:28-30

**Describe a time when you started something you weren't prepared to finish due to inadequate preparation. What feelings did you experience?**

**What did you learn from that experience?**

**How important is it to consider the cost before you begin something? Why?**

**Recall faithful Christians you've learned from over the years. What did it cost these brothers and sisters to follow Jesus?**

In His illustration Jesus was saying that being His disciple involves planning and calculations on our part. We must plan to follow Jesus. We must plan for things to cost additionally along the way as well—unexpected expenses and costs of being a kingdom disciple that we may not know about at first. In asking for full commitment to Him as His disciple, Jesus is asking us to be fully prepared for the costs we know about now and those that may come later. The cost for discipleship is always a cross. For Jesus, many of the disciples, and many of faithful Christians since, the cost of discipleship was their lives. Your cross may be different, but following Jesus will cost you something, whether it's friends, family relationships, reputation, success, or even your life. Or it may just be your convenience, time, and finances. We must all bear a cross. Christians can't get a crown with a cross.

Jesus is saying to each of us, "Pull out your spiritual calculator. Add up the cost. Include a budget for costs to come. Make sure you understand what you're doing. Make sure you have the spiritual capital and are willing to invest what it takes to finish. Evaluate whether anything in your life is hindering you from being My disciple. Then, when you've done that, pick up your cross and follow Me."

**Read Luke 10:3. Would does this verse reveal about Jesus' expectations of His disciples?**

**How does the expectation of being a lamb among wolves change the way you live as a follower of Jesus?**

**How does the authority that Jesus have given us make it possible for us to live this way?**

A hallmark verse on the commitment of discipleship is Luke 9:23:

> If anyone wishes to come after Me, let him deny
> himself, and take up his cross daily and follow Me.
> LUKE 9:23

In this verse Jesus wasn't talking about physical death, because we can't die physically every day. He was talking about a day-by-day orientation to life. He meant that following Him means setting aside our preferences and desires when those desires are in conflict with His. Bearing a cross daily means making the determination every day to choose Jesus above all else. He was calling us to discipleship, not just eternal salvation. He went on to emphasize the fullness, usefulness, satisfaction, and victory that result from the decision to follow Him, saying that those who follow Him will save their souls (see Matt. 16:24-26; Luke 9:24-26).

**What about carrying your cross daily makes you uncomfortable? Why is following Jesus worth the discomfort?**

**In what ways can you be more committed to carrying your cross daily as a kingdom disciple?**

Carrying your cross involves denying your personal plans. It means saying no to your desires when they conflict with God's will. It means placing every area of your life under God's kingdom rule. It involves funneling all of your decisions through His purposes. It includes every moment of your life. There's absolutely no division between the sacred and the secular for a kingdom disciple. Everything is sacred because God bought your life at a price (see 1 Cor. 6:20).

Now you know why there are so many Christians but so few committed kingdom disciples. It's not a club you sign up for or a small group you attend. It's a full-on, no-holds-barred dedication of everything to Christ that makes you who you are.

**What areas of your life have you made off limits to Jesus? Why are you unwilling to relinquish these areas to Jesus?**

**Consider your time, your talent, and your treasure. What would it look like to carry your cross in each of these areas?**

## Prayer

Heavenly King, thank You for clearly outlining for me what commitment looks like as Your disciple. You've made it clear what it means to follow You. I want to follow You with all of my life. You're my King, and I'm grateful to You for all You've done to give me the opportunity to live as an heir in Your kingdom.

# *Day 3*
# PUBLICLY CONFESSING CHRIST

As we saw in the past two days' lessons, being a kingdom disciple is no small matter. It requires dedication, commitment, sacrifice, and planning. But Christ makes one other requirement of His disciples, and we'll look at that element in the remaining three days this week. That requirement is confession. As His disciples, we must publicly confess His name and who He is throughout all areas of our lives.

The word *confess* means to openly and publicly affirm and declare where a person stands on an issue. It means to say the same thing that person would say. Living as a disciple of Jesus Christ involves a willingness to publicly declare and demonstrate a commitment to and an association with Him. In other words, our commitment isn't just to be known and witnessed by ourselves and God. It's to be something that people around us can't help but see as well.

So what does such a confession look like?

- Does it mean posting verses about Jesus on your social-media channels?
- Does it mean telling the people where you work about Jesus?
- Does it mean publicly praying in a restaurant?
- Does it mean handing out gospel tracts?
- Does it mean telling the moms in your mom group or the men in your workout or gaming tribe about Jesus?

All of those actions seem obvious ways to publicly confess Jesus to others, but publicly confessing Jesus goes beyond simply telling about Him. It involves our choices in our everyday lives. Though it would be nice to have a list we could cross off and say we had confessed Christ, the complexities of confession run deeper into the grooves of our daily grind. For example, women can publicly confess Jesus by what they wear. Do your clothing choices reflect alignment under His headship and His desire for modesty (see 1 Tim. 2:9)? Men can publicly confess Jesus in what they say about others. Do your conversations or comments with friends reflect thoughts that honor women (see Matt. 5:28)?

**Read 1 Peter 3:15. How is honoring Christ as Lord a means of confessing Him as King?**

**What happens when Christians publicly speak about Jesus but without the gentleness and respect Peter called for?**


**Why do you think it's critical to publicly confess Jesus in a way that's gentle and shows respect?**


Jesus declares that your willingness to confess Him becomes the marker of your seriousness about Him as His disciple. Being a disciple is much more than simply believing in God. Even Satan believes in God.

Alignment under the lordship of Christ—putting Him in first place—involves publicly declaring and demonstrating an association with Him in both words and actions and submitting to His rule over every area of your life. But for your confession of Christ to be aligned with His holiness and character, it needs to be clothed in humility, gentleness, and respect.

**Read Colossians 3:12. What are some of Christ's attributes that we should reflect as His image bearers and disciples?**


**In what way can living out these attributes enable you to be more effective in publicly confessing Jesus Christ through your words, actions, and interactions with others?**


When you publicly confess Jesus Christ in a manner that reflects and honors His character and attributes, you're living as a disciple aligned under His lordship. Another term for this relationship is *abiding* (see John 15). Abiding in Christ allows you to access the authority He died to secure for you so that you can live effectively in a world contaminated by sin and Satan.

Have you ever been watching cable television only to have the channel go out and the words "Searching for signal" appear your screen? That's what has happened to many believers who don't live in an abiding relationship with their Lord. They're cut off from accessing His authority. They have the ability to access His authority, but the signal has been interrupted. They've allowed the enemy to interfere with their communication and alignment with Jesus Christ.

**How important is reflecting the character of Christ in publicly confessing Christ?**

**Have you ever had someone say something to you, but their actions, nonverbal communication, or character didn't reflect what they said? Did that cause you to believe them or to disbelieve them?**

Confessing Jesus goes a lot further than a simple word here or there, passing out a tract, or posting an inspirational saying on social media. Truly confessing Him as His kingdom disciple is a lifestyle. It involves your thoughts, character, presence, motivations, words, and actions. You may have heard the statement "Preach always, and when necessary, use words." Confessing Jesus Christ should flow freely through all you do so that everyone you come into contact with knows that He's not only your God but also your Lord.

## *Prayer*

God, I want to confess You through the way I live, what I say, and the choices I make. I want my life to reflect You in all I do. Help me abide in Christ so closely that He's a natural part of my everyday life. Teach me what it means to be still in Your presence. In Christ's name, amen.

# Day 4
## JESUS AS LORD

The Book of Romans is a great theological document that Paul wrote to the Christian church. In chapter 10 he included two verses that have confused a lot of people over the years. They read:

> If you confess with your mouth Jesus as Lord,
> and believe in your heart that God raised Him
> from the dead, you will be saved; for with the heart
> a person believes, resulting in righteousness, and
> with the mouth he confesses, resulting in salvation.
> ROMANS 10:9-10

These two verses identify two steps we must take to be saved: confess with our mouths and believe in our hearts. The problem is that every New Testament teaching on how to be saved says we have to do only one thing: believe (see John 3:16; 5:24; Acts 16:31; Rom. 4:4-5). Yet the Book of Romans says we must also confess. So either the Bible is contradicting itself, or this passage in Romans must mean something else.

The answer to that dilemma lies in the context of the passage. Here Paul wasn't instructing sinners on how to become saints. All that's required for salvation is belief (repentance and faith). You must believe on the Lord Jesus Christ to go to heaven, but you must confess the Lord Jesus Christ with the content of your life to follow Him as a disciple. Confessing Jesus means you're living in a way that brings ultimate glory and honor to Him alone.

**Describe the difference between eternal salvation and earthly discipleship in your own words.**

**In what ways can failure or refusal to publicly confess Jesus Christ hinder your personal victory and spiritual growth?**

# THE BOLD CONFESSION

When people accept Jesus Christ as their personal Savior by believing on Him, His righteousness is immediately imputed to them as their righteousness. They're saved, in the eternal sense of the word. But when they make a public confession of Jesus Christ as their Lord, they receive His deliverance in the here and now, in history. Confessing Jesus and receiving His ongoing deliverance are the means of accessing God's ability and intention to intervene in situations in which you need divine assistance, such as external challenges or internal struggles.

The word *saved* means "to be rescued or delivered." The reason a lot of people who are going to heaven aren't seeing heaven join them in history is that they've believed, but they haven't confessed. In other words, they've declared within themselves whom they're trusting for their salvation, and they've placed their faith in Jesus Christ for the forgiveness of their sins. But they haven't made an ongoing public confession, or declaration, of Him as their Lord through word and deed.

**In what areas of your life do you feel you can improve in publicly confessing Jesus Christ as your Lord?**

**What steps will you take to step out in faith and begin to confess Jesus Christ more publicly in your everyday life?**

**Read 1 John 4:15. What's one result of confessing Jesus Christ as Lord?**

In biblical days Christians were brought before the Roman magistrates for declaring Jesus as Lord in their speech and actions. The term *Lord* means "supreme ruler or authority." The Roman authorities attempted to persuade the Christians to declare Caesar as Lord and to deny Jesus as supreme ruler and authority. Believing in Jesus didn't get the Christians hanged or tossed to the lions for sport. Believing in Jesus as the rightful Ruler and Lord did. There's a difference.

The reason we may not be seeing more of God's rescue and deliverance in individual lives, homes, churches, and communities is that we've positioned Jesus as our Savior but not as our Lord.

**Describe the difference between believing in Jesus (believing that He exists or is God) and believing in Him as the rightful Ruler and Lord?**

**Would you say you believe in Jesus as the rightful Ruler and Lord of your life? How do you demonstrate that belief in your words, actions, and thoughts?**

**Read 2 Corinthians 4:5. What does it mean to have a servant-master relationship with Jesus? Why is this relationship good for us?**

Frequently throughout the New Testament, the disciples and the apostles regularly referred to themselves as bond servants or slaves of Jesus. The Book of Romans opens with these words: "Paul, a bond-servant of Christ Jesus …" (Rom. 1:1). *Bond servant*, translated from the Greek word *doulos*, literally means "slave." A slave is someone who has a master or a lord. Declaring Jesus as your Savior takes you to heaven, but declaring Jesus as your Master or Lord brings heaven to you. It's in acknowledging your rightful place under Jesus as His *doulos*, or slave, that you receive His delivering power on earth.

We, the collective body of Christ, are His slaves. We're His kingdom disciples. The job of a slave is do whatever the Master says to do. It's as straightforward as that.

Unfortunately, Jesus has to complete with many other masters in most of our lives today. Remember that Jesus isn't willing to be one among many. He isn't willing to be part of an association or a club of many different masters. Neither is He willing to be relegated to our personal assistant. Jesus as Lord means Jesus is to be *the* supreme ruler and master. He calls the shots, and He's to be acknowledged as Lord in every aspect of our lives.

The problem is that too many people want a Savior but don't want a Lord. Therefore, a lot of Christians today are experiencing the result of publicly denying Christ. They're likewise being denied by Christ before God the Father. Tomorrow we'll look at what that denial means, and we'll identify some ways it reveals itself in our lives.

**Before tomorrow take some time to think about the condition of your heart. If you're reluctant to confess Jesus as Lord, what's the problem?**

**Whom do you know who models what it means to follow Jesus and confess Him as Lord daily? What qualities of his or her life could you implement in your own life?**

## Prayer

Heavenly Father, I want to live with You as the Lord of my life. Forgive me for ways I haven't done so in the past and give me wisdom to change my thinking in this area. I want Your will to be done, and I want to experience Your pleasure. In Christ's name, amen.

# Day 5

## CONFESSING THE NEW COVENANT

Jesus publicly denies us when we publicly deny Him by failing to confess His name. Several passages in both the Old and New Testaments give us insight into the way this denial occurs. You'll clearly see from the context in which these verses appear that the people being addressed are already saved from an eternal standpoint. Their eternal security has already been decided, so they're saints on their way to heaven.

Thus, the word *deliverance* in these passages doesn't refer to salvation in view of eternity. In the framework of these passages, deliverance is God's helping hand in history. Calling on the name of the Lord invokes heaven to join us down here on earth.

**Read the following verses and describe the type of salvation or deliverance referred to.**

**Joel 2:32**

**Romans 10:13**

**1 Corinthians 1:1-2**

**Read 2 Timothy 1:8. What does Paul urge us to do? How did he back up that urging with his own life choices?**

You've probably heard someone say, "I plead the blood." They're talking about the blood of the covenant. However, the way to plead the blood of the covenant isn't simply by saying some magical words. You plead the blood of the covenant by being under the terms of the covenant—by making Jesus Christ the Lord of your life and the Ruler of your world, an action that's at the heart of kingdom discipleship.

In Old Testament times the Israelites couldn't just say, "I plead the blood." They had to put the blood on the doorposts in order to plead it (see Ex. 12:21-23).

It involved more than merely saying the words. They had to place themselves inside the protective confines of the walls that were connected to the blood-stained doors.

Likewise, covenantal alignment under the lordship and rulership of Jesus Christ is required in order to experience His kingdom power, authority, provision, and covering. We read about this new covenant:

> He has obtained a more excellent ministry, by as
> much as He is also the mediator of a better covenant,
> which has been enacted on better promises.
> HEBREWS 8:6

> He is the mediator of a new covenant, so that, since a death
> has taken place for the redemption of the transgressions that
> were committed under the first covenant, those who have been
> called may receive the promise of the eternal inheritance.
> HEBREWS 9:15

> ... to Jesus, the mediator of a new covenant, and to the
> sprinkled blood, which speaks better than the blood of Abel.
> HEBREWS 12:24

> There is one God, and one mediator also
> between God and men, the man Christ Jesus.
> 1 TIMOTHY 2:5

As the mediator of the new covenant, Jesus is our Master.

**If you hold a job, you know what it means to report to a boss. What are some things you can't or shouldn't do or say to your boss?**

**How do you show Jesus the respect, obedience, attention, and verbal honor that are due Him as Lord?**

Most of us know what it's like to have a boss and why we treat him or her differently from most other people. For example, if you're talking with someone and your boss calls, you say, "I need to pick this up; it's my boss." Everything changes when the boss is involved. With how much more reverence should we hold our relationship with Jesus Christ. And yet He's often the last person we refer to, look to, or include.

Our choices have a cause-and-effect element that most of us aren't aware of, just like the choices we make with our boss. Jesus says He must be first place in our lives, and when He's not, the effect will be a lack of His involvement and deliverance when we need it. He said:

> Everyone who confesses Me before men, I will also
> confess him before My Father who is in heaven.
> But whoever denies Me before men, I will also
> deny him before My Father who is in heaven.
> MATTHEW 10:32-33

If for no other practical reason than accessing the power of deliverance on earth, you must establish and declare Jesus Christ as Lord in your life and over your world as His kingdom disciple. You must publicly open your mouth and let others know by what you say and by what you do that He's your Lord and Master and that you aren't ashamed to be associated with Him and aligned under His authority.

Jesus is seated at the right hand of God in heaven, and you're there with Him through His redemption on the cross (see Rom. 8:34). Access His power and authority by publicly declaring His lordship in your life. His blood has established the new covenant under which you're to align your life and your world in order to receive His full covenant covering and protection (see Heb. 9:15).

**Rewrite Matthew 10:32 in your own words and state its application.**

**In John 20 Thomas had been doubting that Jesus had risen from the dead when Jesus invited him to touch His wounds and be certain that it was He. Thomas responded by calling Him "my Lord and my God" (v. 28). Differentiate between the two terms Thomas used and explain how publicly confessing Christ can apply to both.**

I have a master key to the church where I'm the pastor. My key can work in any lock because it's a master key. Because I have a master key, I can go anywhere in the church. Church-staff members may have keys to their own offices, but those keys are limited only to specific doors.

A lot of us aren't able to go everywhere we need to go because we don't have the Master key. We've got keys for certain rooms. We come to church, hear a sermon, and receive a truth that provides a key for a certain room in our Christian life. We must understand, however, that the key to the Christian life for kingdom disciples is Jesus Christ, our Lord and Master. The ability to live victoriously and advance God's kingdom agenda on earth comes through this unique Master key called total surrender to the lordship of Christ. Only when the lordship of Jesus Christ is reflected and represented through His people individually and corporately as kingdom disciples will the world experience God's rule and authority as the Creator intended it to be.

**How do you need to live in God's authority and power this week?**

## Prayer

Dear Lord, honoring You in my thoughts, words, and actions comes naturally when I view You as my Lord and my God. You're to be the deciding factor in every activity I choose. You're to be the focal point of my conversations—Your will, Your ways, and Your wisdom. In Christ's name, amen.

Week 4

# A DEEP INTIMACY

# START

*Welcome to session 4 of* Kingdom Disciples.

**What was a helpful point of review or a new insight gained from your personal study last week?**

**Does anybody have any stories or updates related to our discussion and application from the previous group session?**

This week we'll turn our attention to the intimacy that comes from being a kingdom disciple.

**Who's your oldest friend? How long have you known each other?**

**What are a few key experiences that have strengthened your friendship?**

Good friends are the ones who stick with us. They're there for us through thick and thin. The Bible has a word for this kind of relational closeness—*abide*. Following Jesus isn't about checking off boxes and following rules; rather, it's about deep, abiding intimacy with Jesus Christ. This happens when we connect with Him and stick with Him. Kingdom disciples are fruitful and productive because of their intimacy with Jesus.

Before we learn what Dr. Evans has to teach us about abiding in intimacy with Jesus, would somebody pray for our time together, asking the Lord to open our hearts and minds to His Word?

#  WATCH

*Refer to this viewer guide as you watch the video for session 4.*

Yahweh is God's authoritative, relational name.

When you cultivate the relationship underneath the rule, God shares more of His authority.

Jesus says He wants Christians to be fruitful and productive.

### THREE CHARACTERISTICS OF FRUIT

1. Fruit always bears the character of the tree.
   The first thing you will discover under the rule of Jesus Christ is that you're becoming more like Him in your attitudes, actions, character, and conduct.

2. Fruit is always visible.
   You cannot be a disciple if you are an invisible follower of Christ.

3. Fruit always benefits somebody else.
   Jesus wants other people to spiritually benefit from your life.

Your spiritual ability to take the information and utilize it in the decisions of life turns you into a meat-eating Christian.

You will become a kingdom disciple when you consistently learn to look at the spiritual in front of the physical.

Abiding is the key to fruit. Fruit is the key to development. Development is the key to discipleship. Discipleship is the key to kingdom authority.

The tangible proof that you are abiding and growing as a kingdom disciple will be answered prayer.

# Discuss

*Discuss the video with your group, using these questions.*

Dr. Evans said when we pray in Jesus' name, we're piggybacking on Jesus' authority. How is prayer a means to bring God's authority to bear in the here and now?

Read John 15:1-16. The key word in this passage is *fruit*. What does this word mean in the context in which Jesus used it?

In this session Dr. Evans said, "If you are a kingdom disciple, you are rubbing off on others. If you are a disciple, you are making disciples." Why do you think many Christians aren't actively engaged in replicating the life and love of Christ in others?

Who taught you what it means to follow Jesus?

Whom could you begin to disciple to follow Jesus?

Read Hebrews 5:11-14. What's the difference between a milk-drinking Christian and a meat-eating Christian?

Using Paul's life as an example, Dr. Evans suggested that in five years a believer can reach stable spiritual maturity. How have you matured in your past five years of walking with the Lord?

Read John 15:4-7 and 1 John 2:24-27. What does the word *abide* mean? What's the connection between abiding and become a fruit-bearing Christian?

What makes abiding in Jesus different from trying to increase your intimacy with God through effort and willpower?

How is your relationship with Jesus bearing fruit in your life now?

*Read week 4 and complete the activities before the next group session.*

# KINGDOM INTIMACY

To know someone intimately encompasses much more than just knowing about the person. To truly know someone intimately involves engagement, interaction, and understanding that go above and beyond cognitive realities.

Have you ever seen a married couple who has been married for four or five decades? Each one can finish the other's sentence. Or consider two dancers. They spend hours, days, weeks, and months practicing together to know each other's moves and moods just by being close to them. They not only anticipate the next step but also know how to bring out the best in their dancing partner.

The best linebackers in the NFL are those who've worked so closely together that they can predict one another's moves simply through a shift in weight or a change in the placement of a hand. With the crowd roaring and tensions high, these linemen don't have time to talk to the others to find out what they're thinking.

In John 15 when Jesus teaches us to intimately abide in Him as His disciples, He's imploring us to enter an experiential connection with Him. As His disciples, we're to know Jesus so deeply, fully, continually, and intentionally that our every move aligns with His in an unplanned cadence of connection. That's what it means to know Christ. It's more than simply talking with Him or about Him. That's a start. But intimate fellowship is much deeper than that. And only intimate fellowship leads to a productive, fruit-bearing life as a disciple.

For example, no wife can get pregnant by having a discussion of sex around the breakfast table with her husband. Yes, she can talk about it with her husband every single day, and he can even make some pretty powerful points. In fact, both of them can talk about it for years. The length of time they talk makes no difference at all because no wife is ever going to get pregnant from a discussion of the subject or from her knowledge of sex. There has to be an accompanying level of intimacy, an experiential knowing, in order to bear new life.

Similarly, abiding in Christ calls us to a depth of intimacy as His disciples that Jesus illustrated through a branch and a vine. This week let's discover more about this relational connection with Christ and the fruit it produces.

# *Day 1*
# Knowing God Fully

The apostle Paul gives us insight into the way our abiding (or remaining in deep intimacy) in Christ and our relationship with God determine our productivity for the kingdom:

> ... so that you will walk in a manner worthy of the Lord,
> to please Him in all respects, bearing fruit in every
> good work and increasing in the knowledge of God.
> Colossians 1:10

This passage makes a direct connection between bearing fruit and knowing God intimately. The Greek word used in this verse for *knowing* is *epignosis*. It means "to have full knowledge of." So far, so normal, right? To know God means you should read your Bible. Say a verse a day to keep the devil away. Go to church. Say a prayer. Take an online course on Scripture or theology. Join a small group. That's typically how we interpret what it means to know God. And that's also typically why so few of us truly produce fruit in and through our lives.

The reality is that knowing God goes much deeper than informational knowledge alone. It's not about content. It's about so much more. Let's travel back to the beginning of measured time to get a deeper glimpse into what it means to fully know someone and what that knowing can produce. In Genesis we read another instance of a word we translate as "knowing":

> Adam knew Eve his wife; and she conceived, and bare
> Cain, and said, I have gotten a man from the LORD.
> Genesis 4:1, KJV

The word translated "knew" in this passage is the Hebrew word *yada. Yada* simply means "to know, to know by experience, to perceive." When Adam knew Eve, it didn't mean he had information about her. No, he slept with her. In other words, there was a level of intimacy that produced fruit. It bore new life.

Just as Adam knew *(yada)* Eve and she bore life, you're to know *(epignosis)* God in such a way that you produce life as well. In Him you have all the wisdom you need to walk in the work He has for you to do (see Col. 1:9-10). God longs to produce something in you that's beautiful, enjoyable, and edible—fruit that demonstrates we know God and He knows us. God wants your experience of knowing Him to give birth to luscious fruit in your character, conduct, and contributions to His kingdom. But that fruit comes about only through abiding intimacy with God Himself—through truly knowing Him, not merely knowing *about* Him.

**What's the difference between knowing about God and knowing God intimately?**

**Why do you think God wants you to know Him intimately?**

**List four things you do with or for someone when you're seeking to grow close to him or her.**

**1.**

**2.**

**3.**

**4.**

**How can those actions be incorporated into your relationship with God?**

Intimacy is one of the greatest delights and blessings that two people in a close relationship can have. The capacity to draw close to another person and share your lives in such a way that you know each other through and through is part of the image of God we bear as emotional, relational human beings.

If God designed us with a deep need and a deep desire for intimacy in our human relationships and if intimacy reflects God's image in us, you can expect God to look for intimacy in His relationship with you. Yet unfortunately, God is far too often the jilted love in our one-sided relationships with Him. But He desires the intimacy of a close relationship with us more than He desires our performance for Him.

God dearly loves you. When you place Him first relationally, you experience a level of intimacy you may have never known before. I addition, you'll discover that as you abide with Him closely, your life is more spiritually productive.

**What dangers threaten a believer who's disconnected from true intimacy with God?**

**Read 1 Peter 5:8. What strategies does Satan use to distract you from developing your intimacy with God and from abiding in Christ?**

Satan seeks to interject himself between you and God as he did with Eve in the garden of Eden. If he can cause you to distrust God or turn your attention from Him, He knows the relationship you're capable of having with Him will suffer division. Sin always brings about separation. And separation leads to a lack of fruit in the lives of disciples.

When God wanted to describe what fully knowing Him would produce in the lives of believers, He used the concept of fruit. Fruit is God's spiritual reference to what our lives produce when we're in an intimate relationship with Him.

In more contemporary terms God wants us to maximize our productivity for Him through our connection with Him. In business we would call this generating a healthy return on investment. In sports it's known as a winning game or season. In music it's a platinum album. And in your personal life, producing fruit means leveraging all that's at your disposal to grow spiritually, minister to others, and exalt the glory of God. This goal applies even to what you choose to think and say:

> Through Him then, let us continually offer
> up a sacrifice of praise to God, that is, the
> fruit of lips that give thanks to His name.
> HEBREWS 13:15

**What are some ways kingdom disciples can bear fruit for God?**

**List two areas in which you've personally borne fruit from your relationship with God or hope you'll one day bear fruit.**

1.

2.

The rest of God's creation performs for Him, but the intimacy of a relationship with Him is reserved for those who confess Christ as Lord and know Him personally.

God yearns for an intimate spiritual relationship with you. One of the beautiful things about true intimacy is that it motivates you in all you do. When you truly love your spouse, your spouse doesn't have to ask you to call, take out the trash, do the laundry, pick up your socks, or cut the grass. You do it naturally. Not only that, but two people who know each other intimately are free to be themselves around each other. They feel no pressure to prove anything by trying to meet a performance standard or by trying to be someone they aren't.

Such is our relationship with God as His bride. We obey, but our obedience isn't perfunctory, nor is it a performance. Our obedience stems from a deep, abiding relational intimacy with the Lord. If the desire of your heart is to live victoriously in your destiny as a kingdom disciple, begin developing an intimate, rich, spiritually satisfying love relationship with God Himself.

**In what ways are you performing for God instead of obeying in response to His love for you?**

## Prayer

Lord, I want to know You more. Open my heart to knowing You fully. Teach me how to let go of lists, expectations, demands, and duties and to exchange all of these for the precious presence of You. In Christ's name, amen.

# Day 2

# Good Works
# and Good Things

Jesus spoke the words of John 15 while in the upper room with His disciples just before His crucifixion. This is probably the most intimate setting depicted in Scripture. With His disciples close around Him and with John leaning against Him (see 13:23), Jesus said:

> I am the true vine, and My Father is the vinedresser.
> Every branch in Me that does not bear fruit,
> He takes away; and every branch that bears fruit,
> He prunes it so that it may bear more fruit.
> JOHN 15:1-2

Jesus used a familiar illustration to make His point. The disciples knew all about vines and fruit. The question, then, was how they were to produce the fruit that God desired. To begin to answer that question, we first need to look at some of the qualities of fruit itself.

**Read Matthew 5:16 and Ephesians 2:8-9. What are some ways fruit can represent the good works we're called to do?**

**Is fruit something you're responsible for producing yourself? Why or why not?**

**What are two ways good works or fruit glorifies God?**

1.

2.

Fruit is characterized by three distinctions.

**1. VISIBILITY.** You've never seen or eaten invisible fruit. Fruit is always something you see. You can see an orange, a pear, an apple, or a banana. Similarly, if your relationship with Jesus Christ produces results that aren't visible to others or even to yourself, not much of a relationship exists. Fruit is always visible.

**2. AUTHENTICITY.** Fruit always bears the character of the tree of which it's a part. You won't find pears on apple trees or oranges on pear trees because fruit authentically replicates the nature of the tree from which it grows. When disciples resemble anything other than the character and qualities of God, they aren't relationally attached to Him. They may be eternally saved through Christ's atonement on the cross, but they've neglected the process of being sanctified, growing in conformity to Jesus. For example, if they reflect the values of the culture, then the culture is the source they tap into. Or if a combination of culture, entertainment, self-interests, or even a social circle is reflected in their thoughts, words, and actions, those are the things to which they're attached. This is because fruit authentically resembles what it's attached to.

**3. AVAILABILITY.** Fruit never exists for itself. Fruit is always available for the consumption of someone else. The only fruit you ever see eating itself is rotten fruit. Think about it. When fruit rots, it begins a process of eating away at its own existence, shriveling into only a shell of its once wondrous beginnings. The very purpose of fruit is for someone to bite it, be nourished by it, enjoy it, and grow from it.

God wants you, as a kingdom disciple, to bear much fruit. Jesus said:

> You did not choose Me but I chose you, and appointed
> you that you would go and bear fruit, and that
> your fruit would remain, so that whatever you
> ask of the Father in My name He may give to you.
> JOHN 15:16

**What does it mean for your fruit to remain?**

**List three ways God-produced fruit is different from good works done for ourselves?**

1.

2.

3.

**Can you identify any good works in your life that you're really doing for yourself instead of for the glory of your Father in heaven?**

Kingdom disciples are to maximize the reflection of God's glory as well as the expansion of His kingdom through the impact of what we do in Him, by Him, and through Him. These are called good works. *Good works* can be defined this way:

> Biblically authorized activities that benefit people for time
> and eternity and give credit to God

If you're a Christian, whatever you're called to do will achieve both of those goals. To fulfill your destiny as a disciple means God's presence is being manifested to a greater degree in the world because of your fruit.

There's a major difference between good works that glorify God and good things we do for the sake of doing them. People can do a lot of good things for their own honor. They can feed the hungry, build hospitals, and visit the poor. But good works are rooted in an intimate, abiding relationship with God that's motivated by love for Him and the desire to reflect and expand His glory and will on earth by positively affecting others.

Sometimes it's hard to discern even our own motives because we can't always be good judges of our own hearts (see Jer. 17:9). Despite a lot of effort on earth, some believers will weep at the judgment seat of Christ when they see their own good deeds burned up while other believers receive their full kingdom inheritance (see 1 Cor. 3:13). That's why the foundation for fruitfulness as a kingdom disciple is found in cultivating a loving, abiding, intimate relationship with God.

**Identify a time in your life when you did something good but were motivated by something other than bringing glory to God or expanding His kingdom. How easy is it to get caught up in bringing glory and honor to ourselves rather than God?**

**Read John 3:30. Why does fruit come more abundantly in our lives the less we focus on ourselves?**

An intimate relationship with God is critical to your motivation and manifestation of good works for His glory. Make it a point this week to examine your choices at the level of the heart. Ask yourself questions like these:

- Would I still do this if no one else but God knew about it?
- Am I more interested in hearing "Well done" from God or from others?
- In what way does this choice bring glory to God and benefit to others?

Let the answers to those questions guide you to live more fully for and with God in an abiding intimacy.

## *Prayer*

Dear Father, I want to reflect Your glory and expand Your kingdom rule on earth as it is in heaven. Increase my love for You and deepen my intimacy with You so that You become my primary motivation in all I do. May my life be pleasing to You and my thoughts bring You joy as I seek to serve You in humility and gratitude from a heart of love. In Christ's name, amen.

## *Day 3*

# Sharing the Good
# and the Bad

Intimacy definitely involves passion, of which physical passion is just one component. That's usually the aspect of intimacy we think of first, but it's not as important as spiritual intimacy. Our relationship with Christ as His disciples should be marked by a never-ending passion to know Him better and draw closer to Him. This is my definition of *passion:*

> An all-consuming drive to be closer to and know more fully
> the person with whom we wish to be intimate

Paul had that kind of passion to know Christ intimately. The apostle described it in his classic statement of relationship versus performance in Philippians 3:4-14.

**Take a few minutes to read Philippians 3:4-14.**

A fact that's evident throughout this passage is that Paul gladly left behind his pursuit of superstardom in Judaism because of his passion to know Christ with the kind of intimacy that transcended every other relationship. He let go all of it in order to have what he highlighted in verse 10:

> … that I may know Him and the power of His resurrection and
> the fellowship of His sufferings, being conformed to His death.
> Philippians 3:10

A lot us would like to put a period after "the power of His resurrection" in that verse. But if we're going to know Christ with the kind of intimacy that draws us close and gives us power, we must know Him in "the fellowship of His sufferings, being conformed to His death."

Kingdom disciples are called to share in Christ's sufferings. For Paul, fellowshipping with Christ in His sufferings meant severe persecution, numerous hardships, and finally martyrdom. But it also meant a special kind of intimacy and authority with the Lord that can't be known any other way.

If you've ever suffered deeply with another person, you know what I'm talking about. We'll never be truly intimate with someone if we say to that person, "I want to share only the good times with you. Keep your suffering to yourself."

**How does the act of suffering or going through hardship with someone often draw you closer together?**

**Our contemporary culture doesn't have an abundance of persecution as was the case in Paul's day. How can kingdom disciples share in the sufferings of Christ today?**

**Does giving up your personal desires or sacrificing your ego or wants in order to devote yourself to Christ's lordship equate with suffering? Why or why not?**

Paul once made a very interesting statement in regard to his knowledge of Christ:

> Even though we have known Christ according to the flesh, yet now we know Him in this way no longer.
> 2 CORINTHIANS 5:16

Before his conversion Paul knew about Christ in the sense that he had heard about this man Jesus and perhaps had even seen Him once. But after becoming a Christian, Paul truly came to know the Lord, and his previous casual knowledge was erased because he died to his old way of life and became a new creation (see v. 17). Jesus was "a man of sorrows" who was "acquainted with grief" (Isa. 53:3). Paul found that in order to become like Jesus, you end up learning about sorrows and grief. Paul came face-to-face with resurrection power because he was also willing to come face-to-face with the sufferings of Jesus Christ for His name's sake.

The apostle gave a résumé of his suffering in 2 Corinthians 11:25-28. Paul described all he endured in his pursuit of knowing Jesus. Yet through these sufferings Paul more clearly saw the grace of God. Walking through hardship led Paul to know more of Jesus than he would have known without hardship. Paul went on to speak of "a thorn in the flesh" (12:7) that taught him about the intimacy with Christ that comes through suffering. His pain served to conform him to the image of Jesus.

**Have you ever identified with Christ by suffering for doing what you knew was right or what you knew He wanted? What impact did that experience have on you?**

**Read each verse and record the approach, attitude, or result that should be tied to our suffering with Christ.**

Acts 5:41

Romans 8:17

2 Corinthians 1:7

2 Timothy 2:12

1 Peter 2:20

Why do some Christians have victory while others are defeated? The answer isn't in their circumstances, because victorious Christians and defeated Christians face basically the same kinds of trials. The answer isn't found in who goes to church more often or who reads the Bible more either.

The answer is that victorious Christians know Christ more intimately and identify with Him more fully in the good and the bad, thus experiencing His resurrection power. Intimacy with God, in the fullest complexities of the term, unleash His kingdom authority and power in the lives of kingdom disciples.

## *Prayer*

Loving God, identifying with You in a relationship
isn't only about the blessings I can gain and ways
You can help me. You want me to know You on a
deep level, where we're united in shared empathy
and compassion. In identifying with Your sufferings,
I discover the power of Your redemption in my own.
I need You in my life to help me face trials, challenges,
obstacles, and fears. In Christ's name, amen.

# Day 4
# ABIDE IN CHRIST

We introduced the term *abide* earlier this week. Today we're going to explore this concept more fully. Abiding in Christ is another name for intimacy with Christ. Christ wants to express His life through you. That comes through your attachment to Him. Abiding means just what it says. It means to remain, to stay, to keep the connection strong. It means you can take a deep breath and just get to know Jesus. Abiding in Christ takes away all self-induced struggle to produce fruit on your own.

If your prayer life is just a matter of shooting up panicked emergency petitions when you're in trouble, you're missing the intimacy God intended for a relationship with Him. If you have your devotions in the morning so that you can get them out of the way and get on with your day, you don't understand abiding. If church is just your weekly time with God, you won't bear fruit for the kingdom.

**List three ways you can intentionally abide in Christ.**

1.

2.

3.

**Read John 15:1-5. How does abiding in Christ relate to your role as a kingdom disciple?**

Here's the picture Jesus painted for us in that passage. There's a great vineyard, a vine, a gardener, and branches that may or may not bear fruit. God is the gardener. Christ is the vine. You're a branch. Every branch that abides in Christ bears fruit. In fact, he or she bears much fruit. Conversely, no branch can bear fruit in and of itself. If and when a branch lacks an abiding presence in the vine, it also lacks fruit. Spiritual truths rarely come more simply put than this one:

# A Deep Intimacy

Abide in Christ, and you'll bear fruit. Live apart from Christ, and you won't bear fruit.

Bearing fruit entirely depends on your relational intimacy with Jesus Christ. You can't omit that reality. You can't force fruit to grow. You can't study it into existence. Fruit bearing comes down to one very critical yet simple thing: abiding in Jesus Christ.

Have you ever seen a pear or an apple struggling and straining to become a pear or an apple? Or how about grapes on a vine? No, because the simple act of abiding brings about the growth of the fruit. It's your closeness to Christ that creates fruit both in and through your life.

**Read John 15:4-10. How many times does the word *abide* (your translation may use the word *remain)* appear? Record the phrases in which it appears.**

This principle is so important that this one word shows up ten times in only seven verses. Evidently, Jesus really wants us to know about abiding. The sole purpose of the branch is to abide in the vine.

What does it look like to abide in Christ? A number of years ago my wife and I took a trip to the great grape-growing countryside in California. People come from all over America and around the world to taste wine and see the miles and miles of vines blanketing the hills in scents of sweetness.

In a vineyard the branches are always hoisted up and tied to the post so that the grapes don't drag on the ground. If the grapes drag on the ground, they'll never grow because they'll become stuck in the dirt, unable to absorb any sunlight or receive a steady flow of nutrients. So the gardeners gently lift the grapes off the ground so that they can grow to their potential.

One reason so many believers fail to produce fruit during their lives is that they spend too much of their time settling in and around too much dirt. A lot of people are saying, "God, make me fruitful," but He won't do it because they don't want to be taken away from the dirt. You must repent of unaddressed sin in your life if God is going to lift you up and out of the dirt. You can't hang out in the dirt and also live in the sunshine; those two things are mutually exclusive.

**Read Proverbs 28:13. What are we to do with the sin in our lives?**

**According to 1 John 1:7-9, what are we missing if we say we're without sin?**

**James 4:17 sheds additional light on what sin is. Describe some omissions that could fall into this category.**

Not all hindrances to producing fruit in a person's life occur in the dirt, though. Some of these hindrances are caused by things that are seemingly good and beneficial in and of themselves. The illustration in John 15 goes into greater detail:

> Every branch in Me that does not bear fruit,
> He takes away; and every branch that bears fruit,
> He prunes it so that it may bear more fruit.
> JOHN 15:2

Pruning is cutting away whatever siphons off life.

Sucker shoots are little branches that show up on the vine that take away nutrients designed for the fruit to expand to its fullest potential. Simply put, a sucker shoot is a diversion. It doesn't produce anything in and of itself. It just consumes nutrients with no intention of developing anything from them. A sucker shoot takes from you what belongs to you, thus limiting what you need for a vital, growing relationship with the vine. It siphons off from you what you need to keep flowing Godward.

In our personal lives anyone or anything can be a sucker shoot. It can be a person, but it can also be television or a hobby. Although there may be nothing wrong with that person, TV show, or hobby, when it starts to rob you of what you need to develop your spiritual intimacy with Jesus, it has transitioned into a sucker shoot. That's why moderation is important. You have to create boundaries in your life that allow yourself the opportunity to abide in Christ. Abiding requires your time. It requires your attention.

**What are some sucker shoots in your life that prevent you from fully abiding in Christ?**

**Are you willing to let go of any of these distractions? If so, describe some things you can do to shift your focus to an abiding relationship with Jesus.**

Abiding can be compared to two types of tea drinkers. Some people like to dip their tea bag up and down in the hot water because they don't want their tea to get too strong. Others drop the tea bag into the water and leave it there. That way the water can fully absorb all the tea bag has to offer. When a tea bag abides in hot water, the tea becomes strong.

When you abide in Jesus Christ, your spiritual power, insight, and development become strong. You grow. Just as a baby in a mother's womb gets nutrients through the umbilical cord, the abiding connection produces growth. If a breach occurs in the umbilical cord, life itself shrinks. It's the ongoing connection with the mother that keeps the baby growing and developing. The same is true of our abiding relationship with the vine.

**Over the next week commit to eliminate one hindrance that keeps you from abiding more fully in Christ. Record your choice and pray that God will help you eliminate this distraction.**

## Prayer

Lord, I want to abide in You. I want to know You in fullness.
I seek You in my heart, mind, and soul. I choose to turn
from the distractions in my life and to repent of the sins
I've committed as I seek an intimate, ongoing relationship
with You. Help me hear Your voice, feel Your presence,
and enjoy the depth of our abiding love together.

# Day 5
# THE ART OF ABIDING

If you've ever dated someone you were in love with, you've got a good idea of what it means to abide in an intimate relationship. It's not a matter of a text message here or a phone call there. When people date, they don't just connect once a week for a few hours and be done with it. When two people are deeply in love, they abide in each other's presence on the phone way past the point of having anything meaningful to say. They simply don't want to hang up. And as soon as they do, one or the other will text to say how much they're missing the other.

We know that's true in human relationships, yet we often fail to transfer that reality to our relationship with Jesus Christ. Far too many believers assume that a two-hour visit on Sunday morning is enough. Or perhaps they add on a Wednesday night, a verse in the morning, or a quick prayer when trouble pops up.

But try applying the way you relate to Jesus to the way you relate to other people in your life and see what happens. You might lose a few friends and family members. Try making every conversation you have with a romantic partner, family member, or friend about you and what you want them to do for you, and you might find yourself alone very quickly. But that's what most people do with Christ. They toss up a quick prayer—a wish list of sorts—and then wonder why they're living fruitless, powerless, empty lives.

Jesus wants a relationship with you, not your religious activity. Sometimes abiding in Him will be a five-second prayer just to let Him know you're thinking about Him. Other times it will be a five-minute prayer. Sometimes it will be deep. Other times it will be light. But the essence of abiding is that you're threading Jesus Christ—His presence, desires, and thoughts—throughout all you think, do, and say.

**What do you think would happen if you applied the way you relate to Jesus in your communication, time spent, and topics of discussion to your other relationships in life?**

# A Deep Intimacy

**In what ways do you often take your relationship with Jesus for granted? How can you make Him a part of your regular conversations and everyday life?**

Many people want a microwave experience of God when He's offering a slow-cooker experience. They want to go to church and push a button for quick results. But the truth about microwaved food is that it can get really hot really quick, but it can also get really cold really quick. That's because the food didn't abide in the presence of the heat source. Only by abiding in Christ can you produce fruit.

**How can an abiding relationship with Jesus reduce your worry, doubt, and struggles?**

**Are radical shifts in your schedule required to abide in Christ? Why or why not?**

You may feel busy and overwhelmed, and your schedule might support those feelings. But look for gaps in your schedule and see them as gifts to cultivate your abiding relationship with Jesus Christ. Abiding in Christ is a habit that requires time, but you can begin by looking for gaps in your day. You probably have more time in the day than you realize because you're filling the gaps with things that don't matter.

Instead of choosing what's secondary, use the gaps in your day to focus on what's supreme. Seize those moments and guard them fiercely. He's worth it. You're worth it. And the fruit that's produced both in you and through you to influence others for good is worth it. Don't waste your days in a perpetual state of busyness, allowing the gaps to be filled with distractions. Rather, embrace the gaps life has to offer and discover a depth of intimacy with God that you never even imagined was possible.

God longs for you to know Him that way. He longs for your company, your voice, your presence, and your conversations. The fruit will come as a by-product of tapping into and staying connected with Jesus Christ.

**Read Ephesians 5:16. How can you make the most out of your time to abide in Jesus?**



**List two time stealers you could potentially do without.**

1.

2.


A bulldog and a poodle were arguing one day. The bulldog was making fun of the poodle, calling him a weak little runt who couldn't do anything. Then the bulldog said, "I challenge you to a contest. Let's see who can open the backdoor of his house the fastest and get inside."

The bulldog was thinking he would turn the doorknob with his powerful jaws and open the door, while the poodle was too small even to reach the knob on his backdoor. But to the bulldog's surprise, the poodle said, "I can get inside my house faster than you can. I accept the challenge."

So with the poodle watching, the bulldog ran to the backdoor of his house and jumped up to the doorknob. He put his teeth and paws around the knob and tried to turn it, but he couldn't get a firm enough grip on the knob to turn it. He finally had to quit in exhaustion.

Now it was the poodle's turn at his backdoor. "Go ahead. You can't do it either," the bulldog growled, trying to soothe his wounded pride. The poodle went to the door and scratched a couple of times. The homeowner opened the door, lovingly picked up the poodle in his arms, and carried him inside.

The difference was in the relationship. Some of us are bulldog Christians, grunting and growling and striving when Christ wants us to come close to Him and abide in Him. Get close to Christ as His disciple, and He will amaze you with what He will do both in and through you.

**Describe the difference in a relationship when love rather than law is the overarching theme.**

By identifying with Christ through an intimate, abiding relationship of fellowshipping in His sufferings, conforming to His character, and abiding in His Word, you can live as a victorious kingdom disciple. And not just for a day or two. Or a week. Or a few months. But for always.

**What difference do you notice in your relationship with Jesus when you regularly read the Bible and pray?**

**Although we may come up with any number of strategies to abide in Christ, the most time-tested methods of abiding in Jesus are to read the Bible and pray. Do you have a plan for Bible reading and prayer? When will you do this?**

## *Prayer*

Heavenly Father, thank You for helping me understand the importance of abiding in a relationship with You. Abiding in Jesus is the most important thing I can do. I want to experience a deep, meaningful relationship that brings me love and care. Encourage me throughout the day by reminding me of Your presence so that I can keep growing in my connection with You. In Christ's name, amen.

KINGDOM DISCIPLES

*Week 5*

# INDIVIDUAL AND FAMILY

*Group Experience*

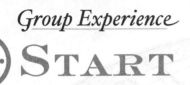

# START

*Welcome to session 5 of* Kingdom Disciples.

**What was a helpful point of review or a new insight gained from your personal study last week?**

**Does anybody have any stories or updates related to our discussion and application from the previous group session?**

This week we'll examine the personal life of a kingdom disciple.

**Share a family tradition you had growing up. Next share traditions you've started with your own family.**

The call to be a kingdom disciple affects our lives in all four realms of God's kingdom. Today we'll consider the first two, our individual and family lives.

Before we learn what Dr. Evans has to teach us about individual and family discipleship, would somebody pray for our time together, asking the Lord to open our hearts and minds to His Word?

 # WATCH

*Refer to this viewer guide as you watch video session 5.*

## FOUR REALMS OF GOD'S KINGDOM
1. The individual life
2. The family
3. The church
4. The broader society

If you're going to become a kingdom disciple, you have to become dependent.

The moment human thinking overrules heaven's point of view, you have rendered inoperative God's work, authority, and rule in your life.

After you're saved, you must come to Him but not with human wisdom.

## THE YOKING PROCESS
1. Companionship
2. Surrender
3. Shared responsibility

The purpose of yoking is learning so that you are becoming His disciple.

The deterioration of the family is the greatest social catastrophe we are facing in our country and in our culture.

When God created the family, He wanted there to be an earthly reflection of His nature: one God composed of three coequal persons.

God wanted us to have children so He could colonize the earth with His image.

The first area of discipleship is not the church house; it's your house.

Kingdom discipleship must be in the home. The church can't replace the home.

# DISCUSS

*Discuss the video with your group, using the questions below.*

In the previous session Dr. Evans talked about the need for Christians to mature in their relationship with Jesus. In this session Dr. Evans said we need to be dependent on God as a baby depends on the mother. How do these two ideas—maturity and childlike dependence— fit together?

Read Matthew 11:28-30. What verbs did Jesus uses in this passage?

Dr. Evans said, "Coming to Jesus demonstrates that you want Him." Why do so many Christians sit around and wait for Him to show up instead of coming to Him?

Where do you find the three steps of the yoking process Dr. Evans described in your relationship with Jesus?

Read 2 Corinthians 10:5. How does learning to follow Jesus allow you to take "every thought captive"?

Dr. Evans said, "The rest Jesus gives is custom-made." How have you found rest for *your* soul by following Jesus?

How do family relationships mirror the structure that exists within the Trinity?

In what ways have we pushed the responsibility to disciple our families onto the church? What would change if every Christian family took the time to teach their children what it means to follow Jesus?

Read Deuteronomy 6:4-9. How is the glory of God designed to be taught in our homes?

What does discipleship look like in your home?

*Read week 5 and complete the activities before the next group session.*

# KINGDOM PEOPLE

I wasn't raised with money. I was raised in a row house in an urban community in Baltimore, where my parents just barely made it. Many of you know that narrative because you've lived it too. Sometimes my mom would have to find a way to cook the fish my dad caught for breakfast, lunch, dinner, and dessert. But despite this reality, I never went to bed worried. The load of life didn't weigh me down. The reason I never struggled with life's burdens as a young child was because they weren't my problem. They were my parents' problem. I let them worry.

Therefore, whether we would eat tomorrow was never my concern. When my dad was laid off for weeks without work as a longshoreman, I didn't stress. I relied on those who were responsible to care for us. I was able to rest because I trusted my parents and lived in conscious dependence on them.

Now as an adult, however, I understand that life's burdens can weigh people down. I've had that experience myself, especially as a young man with four young children, a wife, and the challenge of balancing full-time academia with providing for my family. Yet despite all the stress we carry as we become adults, Jesus says if we'll simply grow in discipleship as individuals and families, we can rest. We can experience one of the greatest benefits of belonging to Him: peace.

The solution to life's burdens isn't found in your knowledge, success, or understanding. As a true kingdom disciple, you access the covering of the Father and the wisdom He imparts as you live under His lordship and in an abiding relationship with Him. His covering and wisdom will radically transform your life and will give you all you need to live abundantly and victoriously with kingdom authority.

# *Day* 1

# COME TO ME

If you've ever watched a baby with her mother, you know that everything this little one needs is provided by the mom. If she needs to eat, it's the mom who feeds her. If she wants to change positions, the mom picks her up and moves her. When she's sleepy, the mom rocks her or sings to her.

Babies are entirely dependent on their parents for their needs. We all started out that way. But as we grew into adulthood, independence started to dominate our thinking and way of life. Although that's good on many accounts, it can also be a hindrance on many others. One way our independence can hinder us is in our relationship with God.

God wants us to become responsible adults who rule the realm in which He has placed us. Yet at the same time, He desires that we retain our dependence on Him for covering, provision, and wisdom. Jesus Christ became God in the flesh when He lived on earth thousands of years ago. Despite having access to all wisdom and power within Himself, He still humbled Himself in dependence on the Father. When desires conflicted, He always chose to do God's will. When He needed rest, He sought out the Father.

God doesn't reveal Himself to the proud and the self-sufficient but only to the humble (see Jas. 4:6). People who think they're smart enough to fix their own lives aren't ready to admit their need and draw close to God. The Lord wants us to humble ourselves in dependence on Him, like an infant with her mother, in order to tap into all He has in store for us as His disciples.

**Read Matthew 11:25. Why does God reveal wisdom to those with a childlike posture?**

**What are some ways we can demonstrate dependence on God through concrete actions?**

**Read Proverbs 3:5-6. Despite having access to the God who knows all and is Lord over all, why do you think we tend to lean on our own understanding?**

**What do these verses say we should do instead of making decisions based on our own ideas?**

**If you've been wrestling with a decision lately, how can you more fully seek God's wisdom and direction?**

Wisdom from above comes with a number of excellent benefits, the chief being peace and rest. Would you like some rest? Would you like some peace? As you grow in your maturity as a kingdom disciple (a man or a woman who is progressively living all of life under the lordship of Jesus Christ), you'll discover that Jesus offers you what no one else ever could. He gives you the power of personal peace. He gives you a way to light your load. He gives you not only eternal rest in heaven but also ongoing rest while on earth.

This gift of peace and rest comes when you do three things as the Lord's disciple: come, take, and learn.

> Come to Me, all who are weary and heavy-laden, and I will
> give you rest. Take My yoke upon you and learn from Me,
> for I am gentle and humble in heart, and you will find rest
> for your souls. For My yoke is easy and My burden is light.
> MATTHEW 11:28-30

**Rewrite these verses in your own words.**

**Read Psalm 127:2. How dependent is God on you to accomplish what He wants or to give you what He wants?**

**How dependent are we on God to accomplish or achieve anything?**

Although God is able to do anything and everything for us, He also calls us to actively participate in His will and His plan by taking steps toward His goals for us. For example, God told Joshua that every place he placed his foot would be given to him (see Josh. 1:3). But Joshua had to take the step.

**Describe how it's possible to be dependent on God yet also responsible under God.**

The first active verb in Matthew 11:28-30 is the word *come*. Jesus says if you come to Him, you must leave behind your human wisdom and self-sufficiency. Have you ever gotten sick and went to the corner drugstore for a self-prescribed remedy, but nothing seemed to work? That's when you realized you needed to visit a doctor. The reason you go to a doctor is that you know he has information beyond your scope of knowledge. He has diagnostic equipment and an investigative process to analyze the data in order to identify the source of your ailment. He has training, history, understanding, and expertise that extend beyond your knowledge.

God will let you use all of your human ingenuity in seeking to live victoriously. He will also let you fail so that you'll discover that the only way to live as a victorious kingdom disciple is through Him. He says, "Come to Me." That's critical.

**Why do you think it's important to come to Christ?**

**What are some ways you can come to Christ on a regular basis?**

Regularly coming to Christ for direction with our desires, thoughts, and needs reminds us of our dependence on Him and the necessity of abiding in Him, as we studied last week. When we begin to falsely believe that any results we get are because of us, we lose focus on the true source of an abundant life.

In contrast, relying on God means putting our processes and outcomes in His hands, where they belong. Another word for the concept of coming to Christ is *surrender*.

Thursday is the day when the garbage-pickup service comes by our home. And despite the fact that I've lived in the same home for over three decades, I've never had a garbage-pickup person come to my door and ask me where my trash is. It's always on the curb. If I don't take the trash to the curb, I'll have to live with it for another week.

Jesus signed you up to receive trash-pickup service when He died on the cross. But you still need to come. He isn't going to force His rest or His peace on you. He says, "Come to Me" because in order to come to Him, you must leave your worldly wisdom behind.

Jesus says when you come to Him, you can bring your trash with you. Not only do you bring your burdens to the Lord, but you also hand off the pressure that comes from living in a sinful environment under the influence of the world, the flesh, and the devil. You bring it all to Him, as Scripture tells us:

> ... casting all your anxiety on Him, because He cares for you.
> 1 PETER 5:7

When you do that, you'll find both rest and peace for your soul.

## *Prayer*

Jesus, thank You for the immediacy of Your presence. Thank You that I'm not going through life on my own but that You're with me to guide me, cover me, and provide for me. I don't have all of the answers, but You do. I come to You for Your promise of rest and peace, Lord, with a heart of humility and gratitude. In Christ's name, amen.

# *Day 2*
# TAKE MY YOKE

Yesterday we posed the question of how Christians can simultaneously rest and be actively responsible in our roles as disciples. Today's study will address that question in more depth as we examine the second verb in Christ's call in Matthew 11:28-30.

Recall that Jesus said, "Take My yoke upon you" (v. 29). A yoke is a harness that goes around the necks of two oxen so that they can pull a load. Accepting Jesus' yoke is a picture of surrender to Him, but it's also a picture of help because you're not pulling the load alone. Jesus is yoked with you, and He's going to take the lead and the load.

The purpose of yoking two oxen together was threefold.

1. Yoking created *companionship* because the oxen were hooked side by side.
2. Yoking taught *surrender* because in the agricultural culture of the Bible, an older, stronger ox was often hooked up with a younger ox so that the younger ox learned how to yield to the older ox's lead and do the job correctly. The younger ox had to submit to the experience, size, and strength of the older one. Doing so allowed the younger ox to piggyback on the power and authority of the older one.
3. Yoking enabled *responsibility* because the oxen were pulling a plow. The younger ox was able to fulfill its purpose through the wisdom and power of the older ox. Like a car hitched to a tow truck, people who are yoked with Christ can go further than they ever could on their own because they're sharing in His power and authority.

**Read Galatians 5:1. What does "yoke of slavery" refer to in this verse?**

**Describe the difference between the yoke Christ offers and the yoke the world offers.**

Many of God's children can't fully enjoy the benefits of living yoked with Christ because we have our own yokes of slavery to the world, to our own flesh, or even to religious legalism, as Galatians 5:1 addressed. We belong to God, but we insist on plowing our own fields, going our own way, and following our own will. We wonder why no power is evident in our lives, and the reason is simple: we don't get the benefits of Christ if we don't yoke with Him.

To take His yoke on you means you willingly choose to go where He says to go, do what He says to do, and adjust your thoughts to what He says to think. You choose to surrender. Your victory as a kingdom disciple entirely depends on your level of surrender. To fully enjoy relief from your burdens, you have to bow your head before Christ and be willing to accept His yoke. As we've seen, you must abide in a relationship with Him and in His Word.

Being yoked with Christ is more than just accumulating information about Him. It involves staying connected to Him. He wants your personal relationship with Him to be not only the most important thing but also an ongoing, continual relationship. An ox doesn't yoke and take a few steps only then to unyoke and take a few more steps on its own. To yoke with Christ is to agree to walk with Him where and how He's leading for the duration of the path.

> **According to James 1:6-8, wavering in our faith produces a state of being "double-minded" (v. 8). Yoking and then unyoking creates the same result. Describe the result, based on the description in James.**

> **Identify an area of your life in which you may be behaving as though you're double-minded. What steps can take to entirely yoke with Christ in this area?**

> **Read Matthew 6:24. What other masters have you yoked yourself to instead of or in addition to Jesus?**

Being yoked with (surrendering to) Christ goes against our natural inclination toward autonomy and independence. It must be something we intentionally set out to do day in and day out, hour in and hour out, minute in and minute out. When we yoke with Him, we'll experience great rewards now and forever. When we don't, we can anticipate unanswered prayer (see Jas. 4:3) and general discord and disharmony in our lives.

Despite the truth of God's Word on this matter, far too many individuals today insist on wearing their own yoke or using their own thinking to navigate through life. One reason this happens is that we think yoking with Christ will be difficult, tiresome, and impossible.

Yet Jesus promises the opposite when we yoke with Him. He's "gentle and humble" (Matt. 11:29), and His yoke is "easy" (v. 30). The Greek word for *easy* can translated "well-fitted" or "custom-made." His yoke has been designed with you in mind. It won't be wearisome, confining, or constricting to you. Instead, it will be liberating and freeing.

**Read John 8:32. How does reading and meditating on truth allow us to live more freely?**

**Why does living by the truth make you more willing to yoke yourself to Jesus?**

**How would taking Jesus' yoke bring you freedom in areas of life in which you feel constrained?**

My son Jonathan travels with me a lot when I speak. On one occasion when he was with me, I had requested that we both upgrade to first class, based on my Platinum Flyer award miles. With Platinum status I'm able to upgrade a companion to first class as well. However, on this particular trip I was upgraded while Jonathan remained in coach.

We went to the front desk to ask why I was upgraded but Jonathan wasn't, especially since he's not only a companion but also my son, and we were told that he couldn't be upgraded because he had purchased his ticket separately from mine. His indicator number was different from mine, so he was unable to enjoy the benefits that would have come from being linked with me on that flight.

Yoking with Jesus Christ brings benefits. Not yoking with Him brings loss. The choice is yours. The truth is clear. Will you live all of life as a yoked kingdom disciple, or will you rely on your own wisdom, desires, and flesh for the many decisions you face in life?

**Yoking to Jesus is a whole-life commitment, not just one we pick up as we see fit. List areas you're hesitant to give Jesus control of.**

**In the areas you listed, why are you afraid of losing control? What can Jesus do that you can't?**

## Prayer

Dear Lord, I want to be yoked with You in all I do.
Although I've relied on my own instincts for a long time,
I ask that You'll give me grace as I seek to further yoke
myself with You. Give me glimpses into the benefits of
relying on You and show me how to demonstrate surrender
to You on a regular basis. In Christ's name, amen.

# Day 3
## LEARN FROM ME

The third active verb Jesus gives us as an instruction in Matthew 11:28-30 is *learn*. He says:

Learn from Me, for I am gentle and humble in heart.
MATTHEW 11:29

The Greek word translated "learn" refers to the concept of discipleship. Jesus disciples you when you learn from Him. It's done through an ongoing renewal of your mind as you learn to think like Him (see Rom. 12:2).

This process doesn't happen instantaneously. It happens one thought at a time. Each time you take a thought captive (see 2 Cor. 10:5) and replace human wisdom with spiritual truth and insight, you're removing the burden and lessening the load of self-will. You're becoming more and more a kingdom disciple.

**What lessons are you learning as a disciple of Jesus?**

**How are you taking what you're learning from Jesus and teaching it to someone else (see Matt. 28:20)?**

What are you supposed to be learning as a disciple? Learn how Jesus pulls the plow. Learn how Jesus relates to His Father. Learn how Jesus views sin. Learn how Jesus values others. Learn what Christ's viewpoint is on a matter. Because we're commanded to teach others to observe what Jesus commanded, being a disciple means we're learners and teachers. We receive from Christ and replicate that teaching with others.

**Learning from Jesus means studying His words and His ways. We looked at some of His words in the previous question. What do you learn about Jesus' ways by reading John 11:6,15?**

123

**What character trait do you learn from Jesus in John 4:7-9?**

**In what ways can you incorporate these particular words and ways of Jesus into your own lifestyle and character?**

Learning from Jesus means replacing human wisdom with spiritual truth. It means learning, accepting, and applying His approach to peace, conquering worry, your value, your identity, your decisions, overcoming temptation, operating in the workplace, showing respect, giving and receiving grace, learning to trust, and handling your money. All of that and more. We're to study His character and emulate it. That's what it means to learn from Him.

Jesus is saying to His disciples today, "Learn My way of doing things. You tried your way, and it just made you weary. Learn My way because My yoke is easy and My burden is light. It's a new way. A new mind. A new character."

**What impresses you most about Jesus' character and qualities? Does anyone you know exhibit these qualities of Jesus? In what ways?**

**What have you learned about following Jesus by observing his or her life?**

Learning from someone requires spending time either being in their presence, reading their thoughts, or reading what they've done. Many people who have a favorite biography or autobiography of someone they admire will read it regularly so that through repeated exposure to that person's life, choices, and thoughts, more and more of what they respect about the person rubs off on them.

Reading God's Word, particularly the parts that highlight the character and heart of Christ, enables us to draw closer to who He is and to learn from Him.

**Read Hebrews 4:12. In what way does Scripture reading help us learn from Christ?**

**Even though most believers agree that reading God's Word is something we should do to grow spiritually, why do so few do it regularly?**

**What strategy can you put in place to dedicate more of your time to the study and reading of God's Word?**

Our world has many problems today, and they come in all shapes and sizes. Rest, peace, and joy are increasingly harder to come by. But when you intentionally go to Jesus, yoke with Him, and learn from Him, you'll find rest.

Two foresters entered a competition to discover who could cut down the most trees in a day. One was an older man, and the other was younger. The younger man's strategy was size and strength, but the older man had a different strategy. Every hour he sat down and rested. The younger man noticed what he was doing and mockingly laughed at him. *He can't even make it an hour,* he thought. *I've got this competition won.*

While the younger man kept chopping and chopping and chopping, the older man chopped for fifty minutes and rested for ten, chopped for fifty minutes and rested for ten. This went on all day long. At the end of the day, the judge counted the trees. To everyone's surprise, the older man had chopped down twice as many trees as the younger. Everyone was confused, especially since the older man worked considerably less than the other. Then the older man pointed out that when he was resting, he was also sharpening his ax.

When you've got the right thing working for you, you can take a rest. You can relax because God's got it. He can accomplish more in a minute than you ever could in a lifetime. Investing in God's Word allows His Spirit to work in your life. Wouldn't it be wise, then, to rest in His sovereign rule, yoke with Jesus Christ, and model His character in your life?

**Read and memorize 1 John 2:6. In order to abide in Christ, what do you first need to do?**

**What three things can you do this week to walk in Christ's ways?**

1.

2.

3.

As a kingdom disciple, remember this one phrase: God's got it. Rest in Him by pursuing an intimate relationship with Christ, learn from Him, and He will do more in you and through you than you could have ever done on your own.

## Prayer

Dear Jesus, help me learn from You and live out what I learn in my walking, talking, and thinking. I want to know You more each day and to know what motivates You, excites You, and invites Your compassion. Show me what it means to live my life in an abiding knowledge of You. In Christ's name, amen.

# *Day 4*

# THE FAMILY IS
# THE FOUNDATION

Before the concept of family was ever introduced, Adam was single. Before any family is created through a marriage, both individuals are single. One area we often fail to focus on in building strong families is building strong singles. A strong single person will contribute to a strong family. A weak single person will contribute to a weak family. Before we ever get family right, we have to get singleness right. Kingdom singles are unmarried persons who undistractedly prioritize their divine calling for the advancement of God's kingdom.

The name Adam refers to that which comes from the ground. God made man from the very ground he came from and the very ground he was appointed to oversee—the place where his managerial responsibilities were to be carried out. For Adam to live as a successful single person, he first had to develop the humility to live life underneath the leadership of the Lord God. As long as he kept that mindset and functioned according to God's rule, he would have the tools to make productive decisions.

The next principle Adam needed to learn before God merged him into a family was that he was to be an overseer. God gave him a job. In addition to his responsibility, though, God also gave him freedom. God permitted Adam to enjoy all the fruit in the garden with one exception: the fruit of the tree of the knowledge of good and evil.

**Based on these observations, what three characteristics of singleness create the foundation for a kingdom family?**

1.

2.

3.

**In what ways does a lack of understanding and alignment under God as a kingdom single person negatively affect a family once one is formed?**

**Read Genesis 2:7-22. What does the title Lord communicate about God?**

Clearly, God was establishing the absolute, authoritative nature of His relationship with humankind through the revelation of His character and name. In fact, we know this is His objective because it's the first thing Satan sought to reverse when he later spoke with Eve in Genesis 3. Satan didn't refer to God as Yahweh (LORD God). He removed the name LORD (master, absolute ruler) and said, "Indeed, has God said … ?" (Gen. 3:1). Satan sought to strip God of His place as absolute ruler and authority by omitting the name that connoted His position. As a result, Satan kept the idea of religion (God) while eliminating the order of authority (under God).

Religion without God as the absolute ruler and authority is no threat to Satan. Life with God is much different from life under God. Life under God is kingdom discipleship. Life that seeks its own decisions and will apart from God is religion. In fact, Satan often uses organized religion to keep people from the one true God. Ritual that isn't predicated on an authoritative nature of relationship between God and humankind is simply legalism, and it's the fastest track away from God's purposes of dominion than any other (see Eve's deception in Gen. 3).

Before any family was established, authority was established. Authority is the key component to living as a kingdom disciple and experiencing all Christ came to offer you. In fact, in the very midst of forming the foundation of the family, God reinforced the fact that the foundation of the family was His own rightful authority.

**Should a kingdom disciple place the needs or wants of his or her spouse ahead of God's rule and authority? Why or why not?**

**What happened in the garden when Adam chose to accommodate his wife's desires over God's?**

**What should Adam have done differently? How do we love and honor a spouse when he or she disagrees with God's view on a matter?**

The family's mission is to replicate the image of God by reflecting His Son, Jesus Christ, in history and to carry out His divinely mandated dominion: "Let them rule" (Gen. 1:26). Personal and familial happiness is to be a benefit of a strong family, but it's not the mission. The mission is the reflection and representation of God through the advancement of His kingdom and rule on earth. Happiness becomes the natural benefit when this goal is being actualized.

The problem with families today is that we've transposed the benefit and the goal, so when the benefit, happiness, isn't working out, we quit and move on. Happiness was never God's first concern. Rather, happiness and satisfaction are to be natural outgrowths of fulfilling God's mission.

When we make God's first concern our first concern as His kingdom disciples, we'll experience the benefit that comes with it. But if we focus on the benefit without prioritizing purpose, we may end up losing both the purpose and the benefit.

**In what way does honoring God as LORD God emphasize the family's mission?**

**When happiness is a family's goal and mission, where is God in the decision-making process?**

**How can happiness be a natural outcome of placing God's rule first?**

Family was established to be God's foundational representative institution in society and to provide the opportunity and framework for individuals to collectively carry out God's plan in history. In particular, that plan includes the replication of God's image through Jesus Christ and the implementation of His rule on earth. Through the establishment and replication of the family, the foundation is set for the advancement of God's kingdom rule in society.

**How does your family live out God's mission in the world?**

**If you're a single person, how are you learning to live under God's authority?**

**If you're a married person, how are you teaching your children to live under God's authority?**

## Prayer

Father, I want to view the role of family the way You do. Families mirror Your love, unity, and rule on earth as they are in heaven. I pray that my family (or future family) will truly honor You above all else. Draw each family member into a close love relationship with You so that we all earnestly seek to know You fully. In Christ's name, amen.

## *Day 5*

# FAITHFULLY REFLECTING GOD AS A FAMILY

Scripture gives us insight into how we can align our personal lives and our family lives with God's rule. It's in our understanding of God as Lord over all that we find the freedom, authority, and power we're designed to know and live out in His name.

As I mentioned, far too many married couples look for happiness as the goal of marriage. And while happiness is a wonderful outcome of marriage, the ups and downs of everyday life often make it elusive. The best way to pursue the opportunity for happiness in a marriage is to pursue God Himself. He's the author of all good things, so when we align our hearts, minds, and decisions under Him, He does what Scripture says He will do:

> Delight yourself in the LORD;
> And He will give you the
> desires of your heart.
> **PSALM 37:4**

That verse is a formula for pure, lasting happiness in homes, personal lives, and all aspects of life.

**What does it mean to "delight yourself in the LORD" in practical ways?**

**Read 1 John 2:15-17. List three areas that are the opposites of delighting in the Lord. The first one is provided for you. Then list two examples of each.**

**1. The lust of the flesh:**

**2.**

**3.**

Delighting in the Lord as a family involves turning from whatever doesn't belong to or originate with Him (the lust of the flesh, the lust of the eyes, and the pride of life) while simultaneously turning toward whatever originates with Him.

**Read Galatians 5:22-23. What qualities originate with God?**

**What area of your life could benefit from an increase of any of these qualities?**

**How can your family be stronger disciples by abiding in and embracing these qualities?**

*Kingdom marriage* is defined as:

> A covenant union between a man and a woman who commit themselves to functioning in unity under divine authority in order to replicate God's image and expand His rule in the world through both their individual and joint callings

Replicating God's image assumes replicating His character and qualities while also turning away from whatever doesn't reflect Him.

**Give a biblical example of a family who reflected the image of God through their actions or choices.**

**Read Joshua 24:15. Considering God's character, qualities, and rulership in our lives, what does it mean to fully serve the Lord as a family both inside and outside the home?**

When Joshua said he and his family would serve the Lord, the concept of service encompassed more than simple obedience to God's revealed statutes. It involved transferring God's statutes and ordinances, as well as the intentions behind them, to the younger generation. That generation in turn was to transfer them to the next generation. Thus, parenting provides the opportunity and channel by which the rule of God permeates the lineage of an entire family line.

In addition to transferring a fear of God and an understanding of His rule to future generations, serving God as a family also means reflecting His character and authority both within and outside the family unit.

Family is crucial to advancing God's kingdom agenda on earth. God so values family that He regularly communicated His plan in history to the nation of Israel in terms of family. He often referred to Himself in familial descriptions like "I am the God of Abraham, Isaac, and Jacob."

Likewise, when God expanded His kingdom in the New Testament through the church, He regularly used family terminology like "household of faith," "brothers," and "sisters." The association of the family motif with the advancement of God's kingdom appears throughout Scripture.

When God chose to redeem the world through the sacrifice of His Son on the cross, He placed Jesus in the context of a family on earth to be raised, to learn, and to grow in wisdom and stature before laying down His life as our Savior (see Luke 2:52). Just as God redeemed the first marriage through the sacrifice of an animal and the covering of their nakedness with animal skins, through redemption in Jesus Christ, families can be restored today when they choose to align themselves under God as His kingdom disciples.

As we maintain the foundation of the family through kingdom husbands and kingdom wives who raise kingdom kids under the lordship of Jesus Christ, we'll see the expansion of God's kingdom in the world through our families as it was designed to be. We'll leave legacies in the lives of our children and grandchildren that will last forever.

## Prayer

Lord, I want to lead my family to live under Your
lordship and saving grace. Cultivating a family life
in which disciples are made and Your truth is taught
is where I want to be. Please help me love and sacrificially
lead my family toward Jesus. In Christ's name, amen.

*Week 6*

# CHURCH AND COMMUNITY

*Group Experience*

# START

*Welcome to session 6 of* Kingdom Disciples.

**What was a helpful point of review or a new insight gained from your personal study last week?**

**Does anybody have any stories or updates related to our discussion and application from the previous group session?**

This week we'll examine the church's role in changing the community by making kingdom disciples.

**If you noticed a change that needed to take place in your community, how would try to bring about that change? What steps would you take? Whom would you involve?**

God has placed kingdom disciples in the body of the church to be His representatives in the world. In today's session we'll see how God is using the church to change the world.

Before we learn what Dr. Evans has to teach us about the way disciples in the church affect our community, would somebody pray for our time together, asking the Lord to open our hearts and minds to His Word?

# WATCH

*Refer to this viewer guide as you watch video session 6.*

The church is God's mechanism to hold back the forces of evil that would seek to devastate a community, a culture, and a group of people.

The church is the unity of God's people to form God's agency in the world to reflect His presence in history collectively.

The role of the church is to legislate from heaven to history. We are God's legislative body.

The way you know your church is His church is that hell is losing and not winning.

If God is your problem, only God is your solution.

The keys of the kingdom are to unlock heaven's answers to earth's issues through the church.

If we're not making disciples, it's not the church.

The job of the church, as it builds disciples, is to infiltrate and affect the community and the culture in which it is situated.

Our job as salt is to be so influential in the culture that we make people want to take a drink of Living Water.

You are to display the influence of being ruled by the King.

A good work is a biblically authorized thing for which God gets the credit.

 # DISCUSS

*Discuss the video with your group, using these questions.*

Read 2 Chronicles 7:14. Why does God always start with His people and not with governments and ruling authorities to bring about change?

Read Matthew 16:18 and 1 Peter 2:5. What did Jesus mean when He referred to the church as a rock?

Dr. Evans said the Greek word for *church* denotes "more than just information and inspiration; it includes the concept of legislation." In what ways is the church God's legislative body to bring His rule to culture?

Read Matthew 6:10. When we pray this in the Lord's Prayer, what are we asking God to do?

Read 2 Chronicles 15:3-5. What problems are you facing that you're looking for a government to solve instead of God? How can we apply verse 4 today?

Dr Evans said, "The keys of the kingdom have only been given to the church." Why is it so tempting for us to use political, social, economic, and psychological keys instead of the kingdom keys God has given us?

On the other hand, why do so many Christians wish to stay in their huddle and never enter the game?

How did Dr. Evans describe the job of the church in this session? How was that job description different from the way you've thought about the church in the past?

Read Matthew 5:13-16. What do the images of salt and light teach us about how the church is to function in the world?

How can your church become a preview for the coming kingdom of Christ?

*Read week 6 and complete the activities to conclude this Bible study.*

# KINGDOM DISCIPLES TOGETHER

As we've discovered, discipleship is the growth process by which Christians learn to bring all of life under the lordship of Jesus Christ. This growth doesn't happen overnight. Even though your salvation is complete the moment you trust Christ for salvation, becoming a disciple is a lifelong process. But it's also a process that shouldn't stop with you.

That's why discipleship includes a developmental process in the local church by which Christians are taken from spiritual infancy to spiritual maturity so that they can reproduce the discipleship process with others. The Bible calls this process being "conformed to the image of [God's] Son" (Rom. 8:29).

In other words, the process of discipleship by which believers become Christlike is designed to be repeated again and again until Jesus has many brothers and sisters who look like Him. The local church is one of the primary locations where this discipling process occurs.

You and I can't participate in this process if we're living as isolated Christians. God placed us in a body of people called the church so that together we can accomplish the mission of discipling other believers. The church is God's place to produce disciples who will then influence our communities. As kingdom disciples think, talk, and act like Jesus, the world is influenced as well.

As we finish our time studying the overarching, comprehensive role of discipleship in the lives of believers, let's look at how discipleship is to be carried out in the local church, what your part is in that process, and how discipleship can affect a community.

# *Day 1*
# THE CHURCH'S ROLE

Do you enjoy microwave popcorn, particularly while watching a good movie or football game? What always amazes me about popcorn is the complete transformation of once hard, coarse seeds into soft, delectable puffs of popcorn. This metamorphosis occurs because the microwave heats the moisture inside every seed until it turns to steam. Once the moisture becomes steam, the pressure becomes so great that the shell can no longer contain it, and an explosion occurs. What was once inedible and indigestible is now tasty, edible, and delicious.

Environment is everything. When the microwave performs its intended function, the seeds of corn are transformed.

What a microwave is to popcorn, the local church is to Christians' growth as kingdom disciples. The local church is the context and environment God has created to transform Christians into what we were created and redeemed to be: fully devoted followers of Jesus Christ.

**Read the following verses and summarize the way each of them applies to the local church.**

**Matthew 16:18-19**

**Ephesians 1:22-23**

**Ephesians 3:10**

**1 Timothy 3:14-15**

A kingdom church is:

A group of believers who covenant together to disciple their members in order to model and transfer heaven's values in history

Like a foreign embassy that officially represents the homeland, the church is to serve as God's embassy on earth that represents heaven. An embassy is a location in a foreign land where the laws and regulations of the homeland apply. It's a little bit of the home country a long way from home.

**How is the concept of an embassy similar to the way the church is to represent the kingdom of God (see 2 Cor. 5:20)?**

**How does your church reflect God's values in all it does? In what ways could your church reflect them more clearly?**

The purpose of every local body of believers is to become a kingdom church making kingdom disciples who are having a kingdom impact individually and corporately in the world. In fact, I believe so completely in this goal of the local church that when we founded our church in 1976, I drafted our mission statement to read: Discipling the Church to Impact the World.

If a restaurant isn't producing great food, it has failed, no matter how good the building or the kitchen looks, because what the restaurant produces determines its legitimacy. Similarly, if the church isn't producing disciples, it has failed. God's goal is for people to be discipled through His church, and the only proof that people are being discipled is that they're changing into the likeness of Jesus. If they aren't changing and maturing in their spiritual lives, that means the discipleship process isn't occurring.

It's obvious when children are physically growing because they demonstrate evidence of change in height, weight, and ability to care for themselves. Development is taking place as the child grows into an adult. In our spiritual lives that development is called discipleship.

**Compose two definitions of *discipleship*, one for individuals and one for the church.**

**How is your church taking an active role in your discipleship?**

In our churches today we can get so caught up in programs and structure that we lose sight of the priority of discipleship. Yet all the programs in the world don't matter if they aren't increasing kingdom disciples. That must be the ultimate goal of a church.

A church can have a number of moving parts, an established structure, large buildings, and a multitude of programs, but if the Holy Spirit isn't free to lead people in an ongoing process of discipleship, the church itself is actually getting in the way of God's kingdom goals for His body of believers.

Churches must focus on discipleship, not just membership. The church must do everything it can to create a large number of people who are prepared and equipped to infiltrate the culture as visible, verbal representatives of the kingdom of God. If it doesn't, we've allowed what God created to act as an authoritative entity in culture to become little more than a social club.

**Read Acts 1–2. What kind of influence was the early church having on the culture?**

**Read Acts 2:43. Are many "wonders and signs" commonly seen in local churches today and in their impact on the community? Why do you think this is so?**

**Read Acts 2:44-45. Compare the initial local church's freedom to provide for one another in tangible ways with the focus of many local churches today. How can the contemporary church learn from the early church in order to make a greater impact on society?**

The early church modeled a spirit of faith, coupled with a heart of giving that stands out from many churches since that time. As a result, the impact the Holy Spirit made through the early church was enormous.

Although programs and events are nice, returning to a church model that focuses heavily on discipleship would bring about a greater influence in our culture. In His Word God has given us the model for the way He designed the church to function. Each kingdom disciple has a responsibility to bring about God's purpose for the church through his or her own individual sphere of influence.

## Prayer

Faithful God, thank You for establishing the church to leave a lasting footprint on society. You've set the church as a beacon of light in the midst of darkness. I pray that You'll raise up great leaders in the churches across our land and around the world who'll emphasize the need for discipleship in all the church does. Help me make an impact for kingdom discipleship in my local church. In Christ's name, amen.

# *Day 2*

# THE FOUR VITAL EXPERIENCES OF THE CHURCH

One of the most dynamic, influential churches of all time is described in Acts 2, which we read in yesterday's lesson. This church was vibrant and alive. It owned no buildings and had no loud speakers or parking lots. It didn't even have a complete Bible yet, just the Old Testament. Bookstores, brands, or Christian radio stations didn't exist, nor did full-time children's ministries, singles ministries, or couples ministries. None of those programs were viewed as essential. Yet this church was on fire because it had the Holy Spirit Himself. In fact, what I often fear for my own church and churches across our land today is that we've essentially programmed God out of the building. In our search for success in ministry, we may have missed the point entirely.

One reason the church in Acts was so dynamic is that it got off to a great start. Jesus had told the disciples in Acts 1:8, "Don't have church until the Holy Spirit shows up" (my paraphrase). They obeyed Him, and the Spirit showed up in great power at Pentecost.

Acts 2 reveals that this church was wildly influential in living out the reality of being Jesus' disciples. It did this through four vital, Spirit-inspired experiences that are necessities for churches that would follow Christ in kingdom discipleship. These experiences include outreach, teaching, fellowship, and worship.

**List and define in your own words each of the four vital experiences of the local church.**

1.

2.

3.

4.

**OUTREACH.** If you're going to follow Christ as His disciple, you must be a witness. Witnessing is the way the church conducts outreach. Whether in your actions or your words, you must represent the Lord in all you do. The believers who were in the upper room and who received the Spirit on Pentecost became witnesses. The result of their witness and Peter's sermon on that special day was the addition of three thousand new believers to the body of Christ.

Notice that these three thousand people didn't come because of an evangelistic program. They came because God's people were overwhelmed by the experience of the presence of His Spirit. They were excited about Jesus. Their excitement erupted in great outreach, and many people were saved.

The early church's witness went beyond words:

> Everyone kept feeling a sense of awe; and many wonders
> and signs were taking place through the apostles.
> ACTS 2:43

God witnessed not only in word through His disciples but also in deed. They demonstrated the truthfulness and authenticity of the gospel in their works, which are the hallmarks of outreach.

**Read Romans 10:14. Why is it essential to tell people about Jesus?**

**Why is it important for church members to make evangelism and outreach a priority? With whom are you currently sharing the gospel or have done so in the past?**

**TEACHING.** Along with their dynamic witness, the early believers were growing in their knowledge of God's Word. They were continually exposing themselves to the information and application of God's Word through teaching. We read:

> They were continually devoting
> themselves to the apostles' teaching.
> ACTS 2:42

The believers were being taught "day by day" (v. 46), just as people were being saved day by day. Do you notice the correlation? People were being saved every day. The followers were devoting themselves to the teaching of the Word every day. One had an impact on the other. To live as a kingdom disciple, the Word of God must be as necessary and desirable for the spirit as food is for the body.

Each of us—not just those with the high calling of teaching God's Word—needs to commit our time and energy to the study of God's Word through the teaching of the Holy Spirit. The Holy Spirit's job is to reveal the Word to us. Jesus said the Spirit would remind us of all He taught (see John 14:26).

**Read 2 Timothy 3:16-17. What four things does the Word of God accomplish?**

**1.**

**2.**

**3.**

**4.**

To acquire a taste for Bible study, you'll have to discipline yourself to sit down and read, whether or not you feel like reading. The more time you spend in the Word, the more you'll understand. And the more you understand, the more you'll want to read. You know you're becoming a kingdom disciple when you're in the Word day by day. Instead of waiting until Sunday so that somebody else can feed you, you're learning to feed yourself. You're reading Scripture, meditating on it, and asking the Holy Spirit to guide you. When the Word of God is precious to you, you're on your way. Church should light the fire, but you must fan the flame.

**Will you make a commitment to study God's Word on a daily basis if you aren't already doing so?**

**FELLOWSHIP.** The third vital experience of the church is found in Acts 2:42. Along with devoting themselves to the apostles' teaching, the believers were devoted to fellowship. The Greek word for *fellowship* literally means "to share something in common with others." It means being part of a common family of sorts.

Fellowship is sharing our lives with other believers. You'll never grow to full maturity in Jesus Christ all alone. There's no such thing as a Lone Ranger Christian who's a growing, active disciple of Christ. It's not "My Father who is in heaven." Jesus instructed us to pray, "Our Father who is in heaven" (Matt. 6:9). You can't become a disciple of Jesus Christ independently of others.

The necessity of Christian fellowship is one reason the church is so important. It's the fireplace where one log touches another and the fire is continually rekindled. In fact, the church in Jerusalem shared not only their lives but also their possessions, meeting any needs that arose in the body of Christ (see Acts 2:44-45). Sharing our resources is a part of fellowship too.

**Read Ephesians 4:16. How does fellowship increase the strength of the whole body of Christ?**

**WORSHIP.** The fourth vital experience of the church is to provide a context for worship to occur. The believers devoted themselves to "the breaking of bread [celebrating the Lord's Supper] and to prayer" (Acts 2:42). In verse 46 we see that they were going to the temple every day and continually "praising God" (v. 47).

Worship is recognizing God for who He is, what He has done, and what we're trusting Him to do. God is the focus of worship. Praising God, worshiping Him, and celebrating Him for who He is and what He has done get God's attention. God responds to our worship, both public and private.

If you want God's power in your life, worship must be part of your daily communion with Him. Celebrate God and exult in Him for who He is, what He has done, and what you're trusting Him to do.

## Prayer

Lord, thank You for the four vital experiences You've
established and provided through the local church.
I ask You to strengthen each ministry of my church
so that it will be more effective in making disciples.
Help me identify areas of my discipleship in which
I need to grow as well. In Christ's name, amen.

# *Day 3*
# BIBLICAL JUSTICE
# IN GOD'S KINGDOM

Each of the four jurisdictions in God's kingdom—personal, family, church, and community—is called to promote justice and responsibility under God in its own distinct way. Biblical justice seeks to protect individual liberty while promoting personal responsibility.

Biblical justice provides society with a divine frame of reference from which to operate. The word *justice* in Scripture means "to prescribe the right way." Since God is just (see Deut. 32:4) and is the ultimate lawgiver (see Jas. 4:12), His laws and judgments are just and righteous (see Pss. 19:7-9; 111:7-8). They're to be applied without partiality (see Deut. 1:17; Lev. 19:15; Num. 15:16) because justice identifies the moral standard by which God measures human conduct (see Isa. 26:7). The government's role, then, is to be His instrument of divine justice by impartially establishing, reflecting, and applying His divine standards of justice in society (see Ps. 72:1-2,4; 2 Sam. 8:15; Deut. 4:7-8).

Biblical justice, therefore, is the equitable, impartial application of the rule of God's moral law in society. Whether exercising itself through economic, political, social, or criminal justice, the one constant in all four realms is the understanding and application of God's moral law within the social realm.

**Why is it critical to promote both liberty and responsibility when seeking justice on someone's behalf?**

**What issues can occur when only liberty is promoted without personal responsibility?**

Repeatedly throughout Scripture God reveals Himself as a defender and deliverer. The exodus from Egypt dramatically portrays His execution of biblical justice on behalf of a group of people who were oppressed. Later, when God gave His laws to Israel, He reminded them of His deliverance:

> You shall not wrong a stranger or oppress him,
> for you were strangers in the land of Egypt.
> EXODUS 22:21

God consistently tied either a presence or an absence of biblical justice to a presence or an absence of His blessing. For example, Israel's worship was rejected because of an absence of justice in society (see Amos 5:21-24). The Israelites were taken into captivity and held in bondage because of their rebellion against God. God had repeatedly told them to turn from their sin, practice "justice and righteousness" (Ezek. 33:14,16), and pay back what was stolen (see vv. 10-33).

The prophets of the Old Testament regularly condemned the people for their social injustices as well. These social condemnations were viewed not only as a secular affront to communities but also as a spiritual affront to God (see Zech. 7:9-12). The prophets specifically instructed God's people, exiled in Babylon, to seek the welfare of the secular city and to pray for its well-being so that it would become a better place to live, work, and raise their families (see Jer. 29:4-7).

**What's your role or the role of your church in carrying out biblical justice?**

The role of the church, as a participant in God's sociopolitical kingdom and as the bride of Christ, is to execute divine justice on behalf of the defenseless, poor, and oppressed. Scripture distinctly relates biblical justice to these particular groups because they most clearly represent the helpless in society who bear the brunt of injustices.

The church isn't to mistreat the poor (see Jas. 2:15-16) or to practice class and racial prejudice (see Gal. 2:11-14). Rather, the church is commissioned to meet the physical needs of the have-nots within it. However, meeting these needs isn't to be confused with subsidizing irresponsibility, which the Bible strictly prohibits (see Prov. 6:9-11; 10:4; 13:18; 24:30-34; 2 Thess. 3:10). Even in the biblical practice of gleaning—leaving portions of a harvest for the poor to collect (see Lev. 19:9-10; Ruth 2)—the poor needed to exercise responsibility in collecting what had been left behind. The amount of food that was obtained depended on the amount of work that was put forth.

The Bible clearly sees spiritual ministry and social responsibility working hand in hand. When the two are properly connected and integrated, people become productive citizens of society while also being prepared for life in eternity.

**Read Leviticus 19:9-10. What do these verses teach us about God's nature in desiring to provide for the poor?**

**In what ways were the poor and needy required to be responsible in acquiring their food (see gleaning in practice in Ruth 2)?**

A strong biblical connection exists between our knowledge of and relationship with God and our concern for the poor and oppressed (see Jer. 22:16; Matt. 25:34-40). Micah 6:8 says:

> He has told you, O man,
> what is good;
> and what does the Lord
> require of you
> but to do justice,
> to love kindness,
> and to walk humbly
> with your God?
> MICAH 6:8

We "do justice" in a humble relation with a just God as a natural reflection of His presence in our lives. Religion becomes authentic when it manifests itself in ministry to others in need.

The second most frequently mentioned subject in Scripture, after money, is the poor. More than three hundred verses directly relate to the treatment of the poor, strategies to aid the poor, God's intentions for the poor, and what our perspective should be on the poor. God cares about the poor particularly because they're the most vulnerable to suffering from injustice.

Ultimately, doing justice fulfills the two greatest commandments given to us by Jesus—loving God and loving others (see Matt. 22:37-40). Christ summarized, "On these two commandments depend the whole Law and the Prophets" (v. 40). Both the content and the meaning of the Law and the Prophets centered not only on someone's relationship with God but also on whether the person was rightly related to his neighbor. The implication is that an understanding of and love for God that doesn't also express itself in love for one's neighbor can't satisfy the biblical definition of *love*.

Thus, Jesus linked our attitude toward God (spiritual) with our attitude toward others (social). When asked who our neighbor is, Jesus responded by telling the story of the good Samaritan, pointing out that our neighbor is the person whose need we see and whose need we meet (see Luke 10:25-37). Jesus concluded the story by exhorting us to love as the good Samaritan did.

**In what ways can you bring God's kingdom to bear on your community by seeking His justice for the poor and marginalized?**

**What ministries does your church have to establish justice?**

## *Prayer*

Lord, open my eyes to recognize the legitimate needs of the people around me. Burden my heart with the needs that burden Yours. Show me practical ways I can help others and ways my church can better reflect Your desire to minister to the poor and needy. Forgive us for neglecting to make biblical justice a priority as Your followers. In Christ's name, amen.

*Day 4*

# THE GATES OF HELL

America has faced a number of tragic storms, such as Sandy, Harvey, and Irma. Yet one of these storms stands out in my mind, not because of the force of its winds but because of the number of lives that were lost. Its name was Katrina.

When Hurricane Katrina made its appearance in New Orleans, the storm was bad, but it wasn't the ultimate problem. Katrina had come into town, done its thing, and was on its way out. The trouble didn't come from Katrina. The trouble came when the levee broke. That's when the city flooded.

The job of the levee had been to hold the water back. If the levee had held, Katrina would have been remembered as just another strong storm in a long line of others rather than as the disaster it became.

God has placed a levee in history. He calls it the church. The church is intentionally designed to hold back Satan's forces that are being unleashed against humankind. When the church functions as it was intended, even the strongest forces can't break it down. The gates of hell won't overpower it. In fact, when the church is being the true biblical church, it will storm in and overpower the gates of hell.

But if hell is on the doorstep, in the lobby, or in the pew of the American church—and many would argue that it is—it's because the body of Christ has failed to join together across racial, class, and gender lines as a unified whole to pursue a kingdom agenda. We know this is true because Jesus made it clear that He would build His church in such a way that the gates of hell wouldn't overpower it (see Matt. 16:18).

**In what ways is hell overpowering the influence of the church on culture and communities?**

**How does unity in the body of Christ help the church reflect God's light in a world of darkness?**

Jesus went on to say:

> I will give you the keys of the kingdom of heaven; and whatever
> you bind on earth shall have been bound in heaven, and
> whatever you loose on earth shall have been loosed in heaven.
> MATTHEW 16:19

Jesus said He would give the church the "keys of the kingdom of heaven." What do you do with keys? You gain access (see Isa. 22:22). Have you ever been in a hurry and couldn't find your keys? That means that you're not going anywhere anytime soon. Or if you're like me, you have a number of keys on your keychain, but you've forgotten what some of them unlock. Those keys are no longer of any benefit to you.

Jesus said the church He's building will have the keys to the kingdom of God, giving it the authority to bind and loose on earth and in heaven. The keys to the kingdom are the church's authority to make disciples and call people out of darkness and into light in Jesus' name. Binding and loosing refer to the church's authority in the world to bring about God's kingdom rule.

The implications of this truth are staggering. If we could only grasp the potential of this reality, there would be no end to the impact we, as the church, could have on our land and in the world.

Why aren't we experiencing this power and authority in the church today? Because we aren't operating the way Jesus designed His church to function. We're trying to use our own church keys to unlock kingdom doors, and we're finding that they don't open much of anything at all.

**Describe the difference between church keys and kingdom keys.**

**In what ways is the church to have a transformational impact on the culture at large?**

**In your opinion, is the church fully using that power at this point in history? Why or why not?**

The keys Jesus is giving the church are the only keys that will work. These aren't program keys, ministry keys, sermon keys, or song keys. These are the keys that belong to the kingdom. So if our churches aren't kingdom-minded—if we've failed to comprehend and adopt a kingdom theology, ideology, and methodology—we won't be able to open heaven's doors. We'll have prayer meetings, preaching, songs, and seminars but no authority. We'll have no authority on earth because authority is directly tied to the kingdom. The keys belong to the kingdom.

The church doesn't exist for the church. The moment the church exists for the church, it's no longer being the church. God created the church for the benefit of the kingdom. God established the church to give us the keys to another realm. He didn't place the church here to be popular.

Our society isn't changing today because the church has settled for constructing buildings and programs instead of accessing the authority of the kingdom. We have church, but we don't transformation. Unless the church is kingdom-minded, it isn't being the church Christ came to build. In fact, Jesus mentioned church only three times in His earthly ministry, and all three times are recorded in the kingdom-focused Book of Matthew. The word *kingdom*, however, is found fifty-four times in the Book of Matthew alone.

Yet surprisingly, we often hear more about the church than the kingdom. We plant churches rather than promote the kingdom. Our seminaries teach our future leaders how to do church rather than how to be about the kingdom. Because the church and the kingdom are interconnected, we must focus on both.

**In what ways have you been guilty of making church more about your preferences than the desires of the kingdom?**

# *Prayer*

Lord, I want to live as Your kingdom disciple in everything I do and say. Please bring me to a new level of commitment and surrender. Equip me and my church to bring about lasting change and transformation in the areas we can influence. Thank You for the power and authority You've given the church. In Christ's name, amen.

# Day 5

# KINGDOM IMPACT IN THE CULTURE

Jesus' gospel includes both the spiritual and the social (see Lev. 25; Luke 4:18-37). It's designed to build God's kingdom rather than to save the world's systems. It's designed to be a model of a different system, one created by God, which provides a divine alternative so that the world can see what God can do in broken humanity.

All the social activity in the world can't solve the world's problems. In the long term, social action is limited; lasting solutions can come only from the kingdom of God because that's where Christ's sacrifice guarantees lasting freedom.

Unless social action is based on spiritual discipleship, it will lack the power for long-term transformation. This is because behind every physical problem lies a spiritual reality. By addressing the underlying theological or spiritual issues along with the physical, we can achieve long-term solutions because we're addressing the root of the problem, not just its physical manifestation.

Secular society doesn't understand the spiritual realities that cause physical, social, political, and economic problems. Therefore, secular society is limited in its ability to influence and transform society. Lasting impact comes from God when His rule reigns supreme and His law of love governs all.

**Name some ways secular society and government have attempted to create short-term fixes rather than long-term solutions.**

**Is church responsible for influencing the culture in a comprehensive manner? Why or why not?**

The apostle John stressed the connection between love for God and love for others when he said:

> If someone says, "I love God," and hates his brother,
> he is a liar; for the one who does not love his brother
> whom he has seen, cannot love God whom he has not seen.
> 1 JOHN 4:20

John reminds us that this love is to be expressed through actions, not just words, as it's carried out "in deed and truth" (1 John 3:18).

James emphasized that we should show this love to the poor and oppressed as special objects of God's concern:

> Did not God choose the poor of this world
> to be rich in faith and heirs of the kingdom
> which He promised to those who love Him?
>
> JAMES 2:5

James also defined true religion by the way we treat widows and orphans.

**Read James 1:27. Identify contemporary groups or individuals who are in positions similar to the widows and orphans of James's time. What are some ways we can help them through action?**

**In the world of social media that we live in, are we reflecting Christ's love when we post disparaging, disrespectful comments about other people or other views? Why or why not?**

**In what ways do disrespectful social-media posts intensify the problem rather than cultivate an environment in which people work together toward a solution?**

Jesus' earthly ministry to people consistently modeled the integration of the spiritual and the social. He taught spiritual truth as He dwelled among the oppressed (see John 4:39-40), ate with them (see Luke 5:27-30), comforted them (see 12:22-34), fed them (see 9:10-17), restored them (see 5:12-15), and healed them (see 7:18-23) to fulfill His Father's will. All of Jesus' good works were clearly connected to the spiritual purposes of God (see Matt. 4:23-24).

When Jesus delivered His great Sermon on the Mount, He instructed His disciples to be the salt of the earth and light to the world (see Matt. 5:13-16). Salt was used as a preservative to stop decay, and light was used to dispel darkness. In similar ways, Christ's followers were to influence society for God.

Salt has been used as a preservative for thousands of years. Rubbing it into a piece of meat helps preserve the meat from decay because salt is an antibacterial agent. Roman soldiers in biblical days even received some of their pay in salt. Salt's value became part of the language, which we can see today in the word *salary*, which is derived from the word *salt*. You may be familiar with the expression that someone "isn't worth his salt." A person who didn't do his job right didn't receive his full allocation of salt.

Jesus put His church on earth to act as a preserving influence on a rotting world, to slow down the decay of sin. If Jesus had nothing on earth for His people to do, He would have taken us out of here the moment we trusted Him as Savior.

But salt can't do its job when it's sitting in the shaker. When followers of Jesus Christ are gathered in the house of God, that's salt in the shaker. When the doors open and we go into the world, that's when the shaker should be turned over to shake the salt of God's kingdom where it's needed. If our communities are going to be better and if our country is going to be stronger, the salt must be at work.

**In what ways have churches kept the salt in the shaker in our contemporary culture?**

**Read Matthew 4:23-24. Why did Jesus preach the gospel in the context of meeting physical needs?**

**Name three actions the church can take, either singularly or collectively, to connect meeting physical needs with spreading the truth of the gospel.**

1.

2.

3.

Jesus also said His disciples are to be light that dispels darkness in the world. Paul told the Ephesians:

> You were formerly darkness, but now you are
> Light in the Lord; walk as children of Light.
> EPHESIANS 5:8

When believers are walking through the world as children of light, the world has a better opportunity to see things as they really are:

> All things become visible when they are exposed by
> the light, for everything that becomes visible is light.
> EPHESIANS 5:13

You know how hard it is to sleep when someone comes in and turns the light on in your face. That's the effect we should have on unbelievers who are sleeping the sleep of eternal death.

If you're in a dark room where people are groping for light and you know where the light switch is, it's a waste of time to organize a panel discussion on the effects of darkness or shake your head over how terrible the darkness is. Your assignment is to turn on the light, and the darkness will automatically be overcome.

Jesus went on to say, "Let your light shine before men" (Matt. 5:16). In other words, carry your light out where it's dark so that unsaved people can see it. It would be ridiculous to turn on a lamp and then put something over it to hide its glow.

Yet all too often that's what we do in the church. Our lights burn brightly inside the church, but we're the only ones who benefit from them. Meanwhile, the world outside goes on in darkness. It's impossible to hide a light that's "set on a hill" (v. 14), and the farther the beam reaches, the more people who are affected by it. Our goal as kingdom disciples who make up kingdom-minded churches is to influence our culture for God and for good. Anything less than that doesn't adequately honor our King and His agenda.

## *Prayer*

Lord, give us the strength, insight, and unity we need
to make a comprehensive kingdom impact on the
culture. Let our light shine so brightly that people
respond and are drawn to You for salvation. Help
me live my life as a kingdom disciple, submitting
to Your rule in all I do. In Christ's name, amen.

Also from

# DR. TONY EVANS